W. G. RUNCIMAN is a Senior Research Fellow of Trinity College, Cambridge, a Fellow of the British Academy, and a Foreign Honorary member of the American Academy of Arts and Science. His previous books include *Relative Deprivation and Social Justice: A Critique of Max Weber's Philosophy of Social Science* and his three-volume *A Treatise on Social Theory.* He is also Chairman of the shipping group Andrew Weir & Co. Ltd. and was Deputy Chairman on Criminal Justice in England and Wales 1991–93.

Further reviews for *The Social Animal:*

"Garry Runciman . . . is one of the most distinguished sociologists writing today . . . To write a general defense of sociology was always going to be an uphill struggle. It's a tribute to the clarity of his thinking, and the urbanity of his style, that this particular uphill struggle has all the ease and elegance of a gentle afternoon stroll . . . demonstrating that sociology can tell us things about human existence which are probably true, certainly interesting, and sometimes not obvious at all . . . this stimulating book is well worth reading."
—Noel Malcolm, *Sunday Telegraph*

"A valuable introduction for non-specialists . . . deserves to be very widely studied."
—Lewis Wolpert, *Observer*

"Distills a lifetime's thought and experience about how modern societies hang together—and fall apart."
—*Glasgow Herald*

THE SOCIAL ANIMAL

THE
SOCIAL ANIMAL

W. G. Runciman

Ann Arbor

THE UNIVERSITY OF MICHIGAN PRESS

Copyright © 2000 by W. G. Runciman
Published by the University of Michigan Press 2000
First published in Great Britain by Harper Collins *Publishers* 1998
All rights reserved
Published in the United States of America by
The University of Michigan Press
Manufactured in the United States of America
⊖ Printed on acid-free paper

2003   2002   2001   2000   4   3   2   1

Library of Congress Cataloging-in-Publication Data

Runciman, W. G. (Walter Garrison), 1934–
     The social animal : W. G. Runciman.
          p.   cm.
     Includes bibliographical references and index.
     ISBN 0-472-09730-X (cloth : alk. paper)—
ISBN 0-472-06730-3   (pbk. : alk. paper)
     1. Sociology.   I. Title.

HM 585 .R87 2000
301—dc21   00-37738

CONTENTS

PREFACE

The Social Animal is intended as a short and necessarily selective introduction to sociology for readers who either, on the one hand, are unsure quite what sociology is all about or, on the other, think of sociologists as a bunch of self-appointed arbiters of the existing social order who are neither clever enough to be philosophers nor knowledgeable enough to be historians. I have tried not to exaggerate our achievements or gloss over the controversies that divide us. But my principal hope is that I have managed to convey what a fascinating subject sociology is to work in. This is not only because it's all about us – human beings, that is – ourselves. It's also because so much more is now known than even a few decades ago about the remarkable differences and no less remarkable similarities in human institutions and behaviour down the ages and across the globe.

This is, moreover, a particularly exciting time in which to be engaged in sociological research on account of the many advances which are currently being made throughout the behavioural sciences, whether in demography, linguistics, and economics, or in genetics, biological anthropology, and developmental and cognitive psychology. The more dogmatic oversimplifications of Marxism, Social Darwinism, Behaviorism, Structuralism, and Durkheimian cultural anthropology are being left behind; 'postmodernism' has come and largely gone, taking with it those aspects of the study of human social behaviour which properly belong with literature rather than science; and a new evolutionary paradigm is beginning to emerge within which historical and cross-cultural hypotheses can be formulated and tested in accordance with standards shared among all the various disciplines involved in explaining why human beings are what they are and do what they do. So to any reader of this Preface who may be hesitating whether to take up a career in academic sociology, my advice is: go for it – there's everything to play for.

My thanks are due to Patricia Williams for her practical advice, as well as to Geoffrey Hawthorn, Toby Mundy, and David Runciman for valuable comments on the initial draft and to Hilary Edwards for preparing the manuscript for publication. I am also grateful to Oxford University Press for permission to quote from Syme's *The Roman Revolution* in Chapter VII.

Trinity College, Cambridge
September 1997

I

A Very Social Animal

IT IS MORE THAN two thousand years since Aristotle said that a human being capable of living outside society is either a wild beast or a god.[1] But what does that mean? What kind of social animal are we?

You, like myself and every other human being in the world, are at the same time three things. First, you are an organism – that is, a living creature born (which not all organisms are) of one male and one female parent from both of whom you have inherited your genes. Second, you are an organism with a brain, and therefore a mind; and although other species have minds too, yours is altogether more complex and sophisticated than the minds of even the cleverest of our close genetic relatives, the chimpanzees. Third, you are an organism with a complex mind living in regular contact with other organisms with complex minds, and therefore you have a social life in which you have relationships with other people to which you and they attach a meaning.

Sociology is the scientific study of human behaviour under the third of these headings. It takes due account of those aspects of human behaviour which are studied by biologists and psychologists. But sociologists are concerned specifically with the groups, communities, institutions and societies in which human beings act out their relationships with each other in accordance with the rules which make them what they are. (Not that all their members follow their rules; of course they don't. But for the nonconformists to break the rules, the rules have to be there to be broken.) Beneath that omnibus definition, there is obviously room for a large variety of more or less specialized disciplines – sociology of law, politics, education, religion, etc. But if there is a single question in which the subject-matter of sociology can be summarized, it is why the various human groups, communities, institutions and societies which there are and have been in the world are and have been as we find them.

There is no implication in this that the 'scientific' is the only way to look at human social behaviour. But it is categorically different from non-scientific ways. Unlike them, it presupposes that the behaviour of groups, communities, institutions and societies can be observed, and the differences between them explained, in terms which can be agreed to the extent that evidence which is there for anyone to see supports the observations and explanations which one or another sociologist has put forward. If you think that this can't be done, I can assure you that it's happening every day and ask you to read on. If, on the other hand, you think it puts out of court what philosophers, preachers, and poets have to say about human social behaviour, I can assure you that it doesn't. The difference is between reports and explanations that you have no choice but to accept, to the extent that the evidence rules out any plausible alternatives, and conclusions of other kinds that you remain free to share on other grounds with your favourite philosopher, preacher or poet.

There are many kinds of human collectivities which sociologists study, some of which we shall meet again: households, families, clans, tribes, sects, classes, castes, armies, schools, clubs, political parties, monastic orders, patron–client networks, voluntary associations, business enterprises, professions, secret societies, trade unions, criminal gangs, pressure-groups and so on and so forth. But common to them all is that their members belong to them in a defined capacity for which the generally accepted term is *role*.

Roles are, so to speak, what they are made of; and to the question 'what are roles themselves made of?' the answer is *practices* – that is, units of reciprocal behaviour informed by mutual recognition of shared intentions and beliefs. Precise definitions of important concepts are not, luckily, a prerequisite of successful explanation in either the natural or the human sciences; the findings quite often come first and the conceptual refinements later. But misunderstandings which are only about words should be avoided if possible; the important point about roles is that they are at the same time *performed* and *occupied*, however confusing a mixture of metaphors that may seem at first sight.

In its most familiar sense a role is, as you will hardly need reminding, a part played by an actor: 'All the world's a stage,' says Jacques in *As You Like It*, 'And all the men and women merely players.' So we can all stand back from our various roles and see ourselves performing as sales executives, lieutenant-colonels, godparents, voters, housewives, mafiosi, university students, or whatever. But there is another aspect to it. If we really *were* 'merely' players, we could sign up for our parts as we pleased, and if we didn't like the script we could turn it down. But we aren't and we can't. Take what is for many people their most important role: as wage- or salary-earners, we are paid for the work we do in accordance with rules which are not of our own making. We may be able to change from one employer to another, and some of us may not need to work for our living at all. But we don't decide the legal and customary framework within which we and our employers operate any more than churchgoers decide the rituals and doctrines of the religion to which they belong or electors decide the constitution under which they vote their politicians into office. Real-life roles, in other words, are governed by rules which the people who occupy and perform them have no choice but to take as given – even if they would like, and accordingly sometimes try, to change them.

What's more, these rules are of a special kind. They determine who is in a position to influence who else's social behaviour because of the roles which they respectively occupy. As organisms with minds belonging to a common culture, we can take from each other whatever ideas, tastes, manners or fashions attract us through a process of individual transmission from mind to mind, and although we may be more strongly disposed to do so if the person learned from or imitated – the 'role-model' – is of high prestige or manifest authority, it is still a matter of individual choice. You don't, unless you're in a uniform of some kind, *have* to wear the clothes you're wearing any more than you have to whistle your favourite tune or read your favourite book. As incumbents and performers of roles belonging to a common society, however, we relate to each other in accordance with institutional rules which place us relative to each other in a social space defined by the boundaries within which the rules apply. Since people can have several different roles, and since boundaries in social space are neither fixed nor impenetrable, the head of the CIA may be a Soviet agent, the President of Pepsi-Cola (Europe) may be an American citizen, and the King of Naples may be a Frenchman appointed by the Emperor in Paris. But within their common groups, communities, institutions and societies, employers and workers, landlords and tenants, officers and soldiers, ministers and officials, chiefs and commoners, lords and vassals, priests and parishioners, professors and students, all behave towards each other in ways which depend on the practices which the rules prescribe for *both* parties to the relationship. That is what is involved in saying that roles are places to be occupied within a rule-governed system (which all institutions are, or they would fall apart) as well as parts to be played (which can, as on the stage, be interpreted by different actors in different ways).

But we must be careful not to flatter ourselves. Social behaviour isn't unique to human societies. Patterned interaction between individuals over extended periods of time is a characteristic of anthropoid primates going back millions of years. Admittedly, that's not the same as what goes on at the golf club or the opera house or the family funeral or the school board meeting. But there are other social animals besides ourselves well able to perceive each other as acquaintance or stranger, friend or foe, owner or intruder, and behave accordingly. And when the smart chimps in the Gombe rainforest start to learn from each other how to make, use and reuse tools and, what's more, to do so within different and distinguishable stylistic traditions, it doesn't sound very convincing to talk about the meaningfulness of interaction between mothers and children, or teachers and pupils, as something uniquely human. Yes, we all have our fully-formed languages and they don't: the linguistic ability of any normal three-year-old human infant is enormously greater than that of even the most carefully trained full-grown chimpanzee. But you don't have to have language to have culture. Language makes us *more* social in many ways – more actively social, more self-consciously social, more intensively social, and more effectively social. But we were social already.

Then is our sociability all in our genes? That depends on how you interpret the 'all'. Many hundreds of thousands of years of natural selection have brought it about that all human beings are born with a set of shared inborn propensities, instincts and capacities of which sociability is one. But along with sociability comes aggression, too, and the ability to bully, cheat and deceive. Hatred as well as affection, betrayal as well as loyalty, and shame as well as gratitude all go back long before the evolution of language. Altruistic and selfish behaviour are everywhere found together and the existence of both is fully explicable, thanks to Darwin and his twentieth-century successors, from within the theory of natural selection. The difference is the enormously greater variation in patterns of social behaviour among human beings – much greater than can plausibly be accounted for in terms of natural selection alone. Take relations between men and women. It is through natural selection that we procreate sexually, with all the consequences for our behaviour which follow. It is also through natural selection that men differ from women in some aspects of psychology as well as physique. But how much that still leaves to be explained! The different forms and degrees of subordination of women to men (or sometimes vice versa), the conditions under which women come to occupy and perform political roles, the success of some and failure of other movements for female emancipation, the range of rules of marriage, descent and co-residence, and the diversity of manners, mores, and attitudes surrounding both heterosexual and homosexual relationships are impossible to account for entirely in biological terms. Yet they are equally impossible to account for on the assumption that biology can tell us nothing about them. In this as in every aspect of our social relationships we are the people we are, behaving towards one another as we do, as the outcome of a continuous interaction between heredity and environment. Some patterns of behaviour are universal: all human societies have gossip and play, punishment and retaliation, exchange and the division of labour.[2] But out of that common inheritance from the long millennia of the Pleistocene, there continue to evolve new and different patterns of social behaviour that succeed each other in an open-ended sequence which is impossible to predict. All we can do is wait for them to happen and then, with the benefit of hindsight, explain them as best we can.

The best way to summarize the process by which it all comes about is the phrase in which Darwin summarized his fundamental insight about evolution: 'descent with modification'. Because, through no fault of Darwin's own, a lot of fallacious racist nonsense was for a time preached in the name of 'Social Darwinism', many sociologists feel uncomfortable about referring to him in a sociological as opposed to a strictly biological context. But there is nothing for them or anyone else to be alarmed at in the notion of 'descent with modification'. At first glance, indeed, it might be said to look like just another way of putting what we already know. It's hardly new to point out that since the proverbial Dawn of Mankind human beings and their cultures and societies have been reproducing themselves in forms not identical with their predecessors. But what Darwin saw was that changes of this kind, including the evolution of social behaviour itself, can be explained without reference to an antecedent grand design in the mind of God or anybody else. As he put it in one of his notebooks, 'He who understands baboon would do more towards metaphysics than Locke.'[3] Darwin himself couldn't know just how right he was, because he couldn't know what molecular biologists now know about the genetic code and the way in which DNA passes down the generations from parents to children. But he was the first person fully to grasp that for the process of 'descent with modification' to come about, two and only two independent conditions need to be fulfilled. First, the basic ingredients of the object of study must be capable of acting as *replicators* – that is, of reproducing themselves, but with the possibility of small but significant differences for which the conventional term is *mutations*. Second, these mutations must have the property of being capable of influencing their chances of reproducing themselves in turn – with, of course, the inherent possibility of yet further mutations. Whether mutations do in fact survive, spread and replicate then depends on how far the environment in which they emerge is favourable to their likelihood of doing so.

This, let me emphasize as strongly as I can, is not the 'survival of the fittest' in the vacuous sense that the evidence for fitness is survival and survival the evidence of fitness. It's a question to be settled by empirical research what mutations, whether in organisms, cultures or societies, have had their probability of replication and diffusion enhanced (or not) by what features of their environment. There is still room for argument about the value of the concept of evolution in the study of human societies – some of it prompted by the irrelevant fear that it will have implications which could be held to be 'politically incorrect', and some by the misguided suspicion that it implies that sociology is nothing more than applied biology. Anthony Giddens, who was for some years the professor of sociology in my own university of Cambridge, used to insist that there is no place at all in social theory for the concept of evolution, which to my mind is about as sensible as insisting that there is no place in physical theory for the concept of gravity. Nobody can deny that human groups, communities, institutions and societies are of many different kinds and that they all change sooner or later from one kind to another. So no sociologist, even those who start frothing at the mouth at the mention of Darwin's name, can seriously dispute the proposition that something has to have happened to cause them to do so.

The history of human social behaviour, accordingly, is inescapably 'evolutionary' in the sense that all new forms of it have evolved out of previous ones, but not – emphatically not – in the sense that change from one form to another is in the direction of some final state of affairs which can be specified in advance: that is precisely the mistake which rightly discredited nineteenth-century ideas about social evolution in twentieth-century eyes. The story goes all the way back to the emergence of organic matter out of the basic chemical ingredients of the universe as found on planet Earth, and forward all the way to the human mind and its ability to build and program computing machines which themselves have 'mental' capabilities. This doesn't mean that the things which have emerged in the course of it are all things of the same kind whose workings can all be explained in the same terms. Our thoughts can't be explained directly in terms of physics, even though our minds consist of nothing other than exceptionally complex molecular machinery. Nor can our institutions be explained directly in terms of biology, even though social behaviour consists only of what is done by individual organisms with minds in interaction with one another. Although evolution is, so to speak, seamless – God did not, one Sunday morning, decide suddenly to implant life into matter, and another Sunday morning decide suddenly to implant minds into living things – the changes which result from 'descent with modification' are of kind as well as degree. The important consequence, so far as sociology is concerned, is that what human beings do has to be analysed at three different levels which correspond to three different kinds of behaviour for which I shall from now on use the terms *evoked, acquired* and *imposed*.

Suppose you are watching a baseball game at the Yankee Stadium. Provided you know the rules of baseball, you are in no doubt what is going on: the batter goes back to the dugout because the outfielder has caught the ball which the batter hit before it reached the ground, etc. But there are still three different ways in which you can look at it. From a biological (or 'sociobiological') standpoint, it's an instance of human beings' inborn propensity to enjoy sports and games in which the participants try to outrun each other, or throw or catch a ball of some kind, or wield an implement with which a ball can be hit. But from a cultural standpoint, it's an instance of how psychologically gratifying leisure pastimes and the idioms, styles and fashions that go with them are popularized through imitation and learning among adjacent and successive populations. And from a sociological standpoint, it's an instance of the workings of a capitalist economy in which professional sportsmen are hired by the proprietors of rival teams out of the proceeds of what the fans will pay to watch them (and the sponsors to advertise on the TV channels which show them).

The direct response of players and spectators to the hitting of a moving ball is *evoked* behaviour: it is elicited by a stimulus to which we react as a result of those hundreds of thousands of years of natural selection during which those of our ancestors who had reactions like these were more likely to live long enough to replicate their genes than those who didn't. The idioms, styles and fashions which attach to this particular sport, however, are *acquired* behaviour: they have been adopted by those who chose to do so from other people, whether known face-to-face or indirectly. And the hiring of salaried players by rival proprietors is *imposed* behaviour: although the contracts of employment are freely entered into, the transaction is conducted in accordance with institutional rules which, like all institutional rules except those framed at a time of constitutional choice, are not of the parties' own making. To be sure, we can't occupy and perform our roles without having learned the rules which govern the practices which constitute them. But although imposed behaviour presupposes acquired behaviour, just as acquired behaviour presupposes evoked behaviour, it is not merely an instance of it. A strike of professional baseball players is more than a matter of taste, just as their jargon and style are more than a matter of instinct.

Although I've chosen a game as an example, I could just as well have asked you to suppose that you're observing a religious festival, a court case, a stock market crash (or boom), an election, a battle, a strike, a revolution, or an office party. Whatever form of social behaviour it is, you will start by asking yourself what these people are *doing* – which means ascertaining what roles they are occupying and performing. But all three aspects of their behaviour will have to be covered before you can satisfy yourself why they are doing what they *are* doing – i.e., manifesting evoked, acquired and imposed behaviour of a specified kind. In practice, sociologists seldom observe directly the patterns of behaviour they are studying. But whether they are dealing with documents, eyewitness reports, tables of statistics, answers to questionnaires, or even monumental inscriptions or archaeological objects, the nature of their task is the same; and if they succeed in it, they and their readers will be left with a validated account of how the particular group, institution, community or society functions and how it has come to be what it is.

Since all new forms of human social behaviour have evolved in one way or another out of old ones, the process which has brought about any particular form of it is by definition a selective process: to a sociologist, history is not just one damn thing after another, but one damn thing *instead of* another. But this immediately leads to the question of what it is, at each different level, that the ongoing process of selection selects. At the biological level, the objects of selection are genes. This has, as it happens, been disputed until very recently by biologists who have held that natural selection selects either the individual organism or the group; but neither organisms nor groups fulfil the conditions necessary for them to act as replicators in the way that genes do. At the cultural level, however, when instinct is supplemented by imitation and learning, the objects of selection are the units, or bundles of units, of information or instructions affecting behaviour which are passed from mind to mind. Some sociologists and anthropologists use for them the term 'meme' which was coined in the 1970s by the biologist Richard Dawkins,[4] whereas others prefer to use the term 'trait' in order to allow for the replication not merely of units of information but of whole complexes of representation such as works of art, scientific theories, systems of myth and ritual, and so on. But it doesn't much matter which term you use. The point is that to explain *cultural* evolution – i.e. changes in patterns of *acquired* social behaviour – you have to have a hypothesis about the features of the environment where the behaviour occurs which have helped the mutant 'memes' (or traits or bundles of instructions) to spread and replicate.

At the social level, by contrast, the objects of selection are, as I've pointed out already, units of *reciprocal* action, since the rules which define the roles we occupy and perform are prescriptive for *both* parties to the relationship to which they attach a common meaning. The objects of social selection, therefore, are and can only be the practices which define of their respective roles. Practices, no less than bundles of information and instructions passed from mind to mind, fulfil the two necessary conditions for them to act as replicators. So it can accordingly be said – to go back to the threefold distinction as I put it at the very beginning of this chapter – that as organisms we are machines for replicating the genes in our bodies, as organisms with minds we are machines for replicating the traits in our cultures, and as organisms with minds occupying and performing roles we are machines for replicating the practices which define those roles and the groups, communities, institutions and societies constituted by them.

Since evolution, whether natural, cultural or social, is not proceeding towards any predetermined final state but only away from what may, for the moment, be a more or less stable equilibrium, it will never be any more possible for sociologists to predict the future of institutions and societies than for anthropologists to predict the future of cultures or biologists to predict the future of species. In the words of the American demographer Joel E. Cohen's only half-joking Law of Prediction, 'The more confidence someone places in an unconditional prediction of what will happen in human affairs, the less confidence we should place in that prediction.'[5] The problem is not just the incalculability of the consequences of the interaction of an enormous multiplicity of separate events. It's also that, as the philosopher Karl Popper has argued to particular effect, to predict the future state of human societies would involve, among other things, predicting the future of sociological knowledge itself, and there is no way in which we can claim already to know what we have yet to discover. Critics of sociology sometimes argue that because sociologists can't predict how future societies will evolve it isn't really a science at all. But then they will have to say the same about biology and its inability to predict the future evolution of species. If what distinguishes science from non-science is that its conclusions are prescriptive for all observers in accordance with the strength of evidence which they can all go and check for themselves, there is no argument whatever for dismissing explanations which can be tested only with hindsight as 'unscientific'. Sherlock Holmes can't *predict* the clues which will enable him to solve the crime; but when he follows up the clues which do indeed solve it, his solution is no less 'scientific' than if he had conducted a laboratory experiment whose outcome he had specified in advance.

On the other hand, it would obviously be a mistake to argue that human social behaviour isn't predictable at all. How else, for a start, do advertisers grow rich? We are successfully predicting each other's social behaviour every day of the week, and the continuance of the cultures and societies to which we belong depends on our ability to do so. If you and I are introduced to each other on a social occasion, I am at least as sure that if I hold out my hand you will shake it as I am that if I depress the accelerator pedal of my car it will start to go faster. We wouldn't be the very social animal that we are unless we could rely on each other's responses to each other's behaviour for most of the time. When somebody's social behaviour is totally and consistently unpredictable, we can tell at once that we are confronted with one of Aristotle's wild beasts or gods. A society in which nobody's behaviour was predictable wouldn't be a society at all.

But wait a minute. Suppose that in order to justify what I've said in the preceding paragraph I am rash enough to bet you $100 that if I hold out my hand to Joe Soap, whom I've never previously met, he will shake it as our respective roles and the conventions of our common culture dictate. Your ploy is obvious. All you have to do is take Joe on one side and offer him $50 (or, if he is the kind of organism with a complex mind who turns out to be a really tough bargainer, $99) to keep his hands to his sides. This isn't as stupid an example as it looks. It brings out just as clearly as a more serious-looking example would do the implications for the scientific study of human social behaviour of the familiar fact that most of it is a matter of purposes and goals and self-conscious decisions to pursue them. From this, some sociologists have concluded not merely that predictions about human behaviour can be overturned in ways that predictions about inanimate objects can't, but also that the only way to explain human behaviour is for the observer to reproduce in his or her own mind what is going on in the minds of the people whose purposes and goals are dictating their behaviour. This second conclusion, however, is right in one sense but wrong in another. It's right in the sense that for me to explain what you're doing, I do have to know what you *are* doing. If I think you're *really* trying to throttle your little school-fellow when it's only a game you're playing, my research project about the social behaviour of young adolescents in educational institutions isn't going to get very far, just as if I think you *really* believe that the spirits of your ancestors can somehow influence what happens in your own life when you're only performing what you know to be a purely symbolic ritual at their gravesides, I shan't be a very good sociologist of religion. But it's wrong in the sense that it mustn't be supposed that this makes the explanation of behaviour into an exercise of a quite different kind. It doesn't. The question 'what made you decide to pursue your chosen objective and act accordingly?' can be addressed by the same methods, and the answer assessed by the same criteria, as the question 'what made you respond instinctively to what you heard and saw in the way that you did?' The fact of our self-awareness of our acquired and imposed behaviour doesn't affect one way or the other the validity of the explanation of the behaviour of which our behaving selves are aware. What matters is that the researcher who is doing the explaining should know what's going on – that is, should have identified the intention which makes the action what it is before going on to identify the motive which lies behind it and the environmental conditions which have brought that rather than another motive into play. The !Kung San of the Kalahari Desert are as aware as are the professors and graduate students who study them of the function of meat-sharing in reinforcing their social ties. But the function would be the same even if they weren't.

Many people find this way of looking at human behaviour counter-intuitive because it seems more natural to look for the reasons which we have for our decisions than for external influences which we are able, if we so choose, to resist or ignore. But the antithesis is a false one. The concepts of social selection and environmental pressure are not in contradiction with the concepts of individual decision and rational choice. On the contrary, there is every reason to suppose that the human mind has been programmed by natural selection to calculate the trade-off between the costs and the benefits of one course of action rather than another. But although our imposed as well as our acquired behaviour is therefore a 'matter of choice' – the only thing we all have to do is die, and as Wittgenstein said, death isn't an event in life – to say so explains neither the cause of the choice (and thereby the behaviour) nor its consequences. The question 'with what conscious purpose in mind was this mutation in social behaviour introduced?' is quite compatible with, but leaves still to be answered, the question 'how did this mutation affect the subsequent evolution of the society in which it occurred?' Let me give an example from military history. The rulers and generals of seventeenth-century Europe who first introduced infantry drill into the training of their previously undisciplined recruits had a clear idea of what they wished it to achieve and of how it would serve their interests, both personal and patriotic, if it did. What's more, they had an evident inkling of the biological as well as sociological reasons for why they were right: as the famous Maréchal de Saxe, among others, was aware, men marching in step in close formation to the sound of music respond instinctively in a way which makes them more effective on the field of battle. But although the innovators succeeded in their aim – which is more than most innovators do – it's not their desire to win wars and battles which explains their success. To explain *that*, and the consequent changes in how European wars were fought, it has to be shown why they were right – which means showing what competitive advantage was conferred by the adoption of this novel set of practices on the soldiers trained in it, the armies manned by those soldiers, and the states whose armies they were.[6]

'Then if sociology can explain why people choose between alternative patterns of social behaviour in the way that they do, does this not amount to a claim that sociology is a predictive science after all?' No, not *truly* predictive. A prediction, to deserve the name, has to be more than a guess which turns out to be right. There may be any number of twentieth-century sociologists who can claim to have said in advance that, say, the economy of the Soviet Union would collapse sooner or later, or the British Labour Party would be out of power for several general elections after 1979, or a resurgent Islam would pose an increasing threat to the political stability of the Arab states. But for a guess to be turned into a prediction, the conditions which, if they hold good, will produce the predicted outcome at the predicted time and place have to be specified. And if you think that's easy to do, just give it a try. An article in the journal *Contention* in the issue for the winter of 1993 by Jack B. Goldstone is called 'Predicting Revolutions: why we could (and should) have foreseen the Revolutions of 1989–91 in the USSR and Eastern Europe'.[7] So maybe you could, Jack. And if you could, you should. But you didn't.

Nobody is going to pretend that the most brilliant economist who ever lived could predict what the prices are going to be on the New York Stock Exchange a year ahead. Just imagine what would be happening on the traders' screens if a consortium of investors somewhere had a software package that could do *that* for them! But economists may be able to predict the conditions under which commodity prices will rise or the marginal cost of a product's entry into a new market will fall, and even (maybe) the conditions under which the stock market will move up or down in the short term. Similarly, not even the most brilliant political scientist who ever lived could predict what the distribution of seats will be in the British House of Commons or the American Congress in fifty years' time. But political scientists armed with the results of sample surveys are quite good at predicting the outcome of a general election to within one or two per cent of the popular vote at the start of the campaign. Even sociologists may succeed in making *some* predictions which aren't *just* guesses. But could any sociologist have predicted when and how the fall of the Roman Empire, the rise of Islam, the Spanish conquest of what thereby came to be known as 'Hispanic' America, or the evolution of industrial capitalism out of agricultural feudalism were going to happen? Of course not – no more than a biologist surveying the world five million years ago, when our ancestors were first diverging, genetically speaking, from the chimps, could have predicted when and how it would one day come to be dominated by *Homo sapiens*, i.e. us.

This may seem to imply that the more specialized social sciences gain their apparent ability to frame more accurate predictions at the price of increasing remoteness from the recalcitrant facts of actual social behaviour. What, for example, do economists have to say about buyers of luxury goods who knowingly pay more for less? What do political scientists have to say about voters who are motivated entirely by the candidate's looks? But there is nothing inherently inexplicable about decisions like these, and nothing in the explanations of the resulting behaviour put forward by economists and political scientists which is incompatible with anything said in this chapter. This book will touch on the specialized social sciences only in passing. But that doesn't mean that they have less interesting things to say about human social behaviour than sociology itself. What is 'interesting' is, to be sure, a subjective matter which we all have to settle for ourselves. But many practitioners of many different social sciences have produced explanations of patterns of human social behaviour which are much more than abstract constructions about idealized human beings and which have withstood attempted refutation just as well as anything sociologists have found out about groups, communities, institutions and societies as such. Besides, we sociologists need all the help we can get, from biologists, psychologists, historians and even philosophers no less than from practitioners of the specialized social sciences whose concerns overlap with our own.

One last preliminary point. I hope that no reader of this paragraph will dispute that explanations of why the world is as it is are logically independent of value-judgements about whether the state of the world is good or bad. If it's true that the Normans conquered England in 1066 because King Harold was killed by an arrow in his eye at the Battle of Hastings, the conclusion stands whether or not you or anybody else thinks that the Norman Conquest was a good (or bad) thing. But readers of sociology books often find that they are being treated to both. Nor should this come as a surprise. Sociologists, like everybody else, have and can't help having views of their own about the kinds of institutions, forms of social behaviour, and performances of individual roles which are to be admired or deplored, and their approaches to the study of them may well be influenced by those views. But that makes no difference to the validity of their competing explanations of why human groups, communities, institutions and societies are as they are, any more than the moral, political or aesthetic values of geologists make a difference to the validity (or not) of their competing explanations of why the continents and oceans of the earth are as they are. True, nineteenth-century geologists *were* influenced, among other things, by their different interpretations of the Book of Genesis. True, too, you can and probably do have a view about the morality of capitalism which you can hardly have about the morality of continental drift. But whether the causes and consequences of capitalism are what, according to your moral, political or religious views, you would wish them to be is something you must decide for yourself on other grounds. And if somebody says, 'But look at how much sociological writing is blatantly biased against (or in favour of) capitalism (or socialism)!', the answer is: 'No doubt; but the fact that bias of this kind can be detected is itself a conclusive demonstration that the author's values are logically distinct from the hypotheses of cause and effect of whose validity the same author is trying to persuade you as well.'

That being so, it comes as something of a surprise (at least to me) to find a distinguished British historian of medicine, Professor Roy Porter, quoted by the *Times Higher Education Supplement* in 1995 as saying that he can't help feeling that the increasing recent success of evolutionary theory is 'a political project'. But on reflection, I think I know what he means. It is undeniably true of science, both natural and social, that it *can* have political consequences and that its practitioners *may* themselves have political motives. Darwinian theory *has* been used, or rather misused, for political purposes, and if you are worried that the discoveries of either natural or social science may be invoked in furtherance of ends which you deplore you are fully entitled to wish that scientists would stop trying to make them. But that does nothing to undermine their claims to be doing science. On the contrary: it is when their findings *do* succeed in withstanding attempted refutation that their possible political uses become a threat to those with whose interests and purposes they conflict. When in the early seventeenth century the Vatican was getting uptight about Galileo and his

II

What Exactly Do You Want to Know?

EVEN BEFORE OUR remote ancestors were in contact with the extinct people whom we now call 'Neanderthals', people of one kind, or in one group, or from one territory, have been curious about the behaviour of people other than themselves. Much of the curiosity is about their acquired behaviour: why do they wear such funny hats? how can they bear to eat that meat raw? what on earth are those pictures they're painting all about? But questions about their imposed behaviour will occur no less readily to trained and untrained observers alike: how do they choose their leaders? what is the distribution of property among them? what are they either required or forbidden to do by the incumbents of roles with the power to see to it that they do?

Herodotus, the so-called 'father of history', can at least as plausibly be called the father of sociology. His famous book, written in the mid-fifth century BC, is primarily concerned to narrate the victory of the mainland Greeks over the invading Persians. But it is also a rich and fascinating repository of observations about other peoples, obtained by extensive travel and systematic analysis of oral traditions, eyewitness accounts and physical records. Although he does appear to have believed some things which he shouldn't, such as that the walls of Babylon were 200 'royal cubits' (300 feet!) high, it's remarkable how often his account has been subsequently confirmed – in the most spectacular instance, by archaeological evidence about Scythian burial customs discovered less than half a century ago. What's more, he articulates precisely the two fundamental aspects of all sociological enquiry: the recognition that every society is different from every other, but that all are at the same time variants of a universal human nature. Although, as Herodotus explicitly remarks, the members of all societies are inclined to take their own as the paradigm, none are any more entitled to do so than any others, however strongly they believe, now as then, that they are.[1]

It follows from Herodotus's approach that there are two different but equally valid responses which the members of one society will have to what they find out about another: 'how unlike us they are!' – yes, but at the same time: 'how recognizable!' Admittedly, all such comparisons have to start from somewhere – in the case of Herodotus, from the viewpoint of a Greek looking at non-Greeks – and different observers will always be interested in, and surprised by, different things. Thus: 'They not only *kill* their prisoners of war but *eat* them!', or '*Black* people are treated differently from *white* people over there!', or 'The *state* owns all the factories *as well as* the land!', or 'Would you believe it – in ancient Mesopotamia a *nun* could be a *businesswoman*, and in Anglo-Saxon England a *priest* could be a *slave!*' But equally: 'They admire successful athletes just like we do!', or 'Look how those late Roman bureaucrats behaved – no differently from ours!'[2]

Whatever the contrast being drawn between 'our' roles and 'theirs', sociologists owe it both to their readers and to themselves to get their basic observations right. This isn't always as easy as it may seem. For a start, there is the language problem: if an English-speaking sociologist asks a French-speaking informant about the role of the informant's boss, the English-speaking sociologist must beware of equating '*patron*', which *is* what English speakers mean by 'boss', with 'patron', which isn't. But even when both the sociologist and the native informant understand correctly what the other is saying, the sociologist may be misled by having failed to ask the right question. When Captain R. S. Rattray, a British colonial officer who had spent many years among the Ashanti of what was then, in the 1910s and '20s, called the Gold Coast, asked his native informants why he had never been told that the Queen Mother used to outrank the King, they replied: 'The white man never asked us this; you have dealings with and recognize only the men; we supposed the Europeans considered women of no account and we know you do not recognize them as we have always done.'³

This sort of experience is disconcerting enough. But even if the sociologist has asked all the right questions, the questions may not have been asked of the right people. Or the right people may, for reasons of their own, have given the wrong answers. A classic example is the account of female adolescence in Samoa by the American anthropologist Margaret Mead. Her account, which was uncritically accepted by an enormous readership for several decades after its publication in 1928, depicted a guilt-free world of permissive sexuality. But Mead had no detailed knowledge of Samoan society and language, she didn't check what she was told by her 25 young informants against either direct observations of her own or alternative accounts by other, adult Samoans, and it never seems to have occurred to her that she might be being deliberately misled. It is, accordingly, no surprise that she should turn out to have got it quite badly wrong. The surprise is that it took so long for her mistakes to be diagnosed by other observers.⁴ But there are many other instances where researchers whose intellectual honesty (as opposed to their judgement) is not in doubt have applied themselves to explaining something which was never there to be explained – for example, explaining the emergence of 'nuclear' households of parents and children by contrast with a purely presumptive 'extended family' pattern attributed to the pre-industrial past, or explaining 'new' working-class lifestyles by contrast with a purely presumptive 'proletarian' culture attributed to nineteenth-century industrialization. Or take Captain Archibald Blair, who reported on the basis of an exploration carried out in 1789 that chiefs in the Andaman Islands were 'generally painted red'. Nice try, Captain. But as the British anthropologist A. R. Radcliffe-Brown discovered a little over a century later, the Andaman Islanders don't have any chiefs.[5]

The difficult cases can be very difficult indeed. A notoriously intriguing one is the reception of yet another Captain (Cook this time) by the Hawaiian Islanders when he arrived there on board HMS *Resolution* in 1778. Did they or didn't they regard him as a god? The American anthropologist Marshall Sahlins is sure that they did, given that Cook's appearance was entirely consistent with their beliefs and expectations and that they had no previous direct acquaintance with Europeans. But the Sri Lankan anthropologist Gananath Obeyesekere is sure that they didn't; what they did (or so Obeyesekere believes) is deify him for their own political purposes after he had been killed in a scuffle which broke out during his third and unexpected visit. It's a particularly difficult case for two reasons. First, the evidence, both historical and anthropological, is ambiguous and incomplete. But second, the question is such as to stir up just the kind of accusations of intellectual bad faith as in fact it has. For Obeyesekere, Sahlins is imposing on the natives of eighteenth-century Hawaii a white imperialist myth about their propensity to see visiting Europeans as gods. For Sahlins, Obeyesekere is imposing on them a myth of universal (but really only bourgeois European) rationalism which denies them their own coherent and distinctive culture. So far, at least, Sahlins seems to have had the better of the argument.[6] But that's not the point. The point is that if we could go back in time, check out the evidence as it has come down to us, interview the people involved, and observe how they actually behaved, we'd know for sure. The conclusion to be drawn isn't that arguments of this sort are difficult to settle conclusively (they are), or that they can be used to fight ideological battles of the here and now (they can), or that they touch on deep philosophical issues about the nature of religious belief (they do). It's that for all that, they are amenable in principle to empirical research.

Nor is it as if the issue is so difficult to resolve because of the distance in time and space between twentieth-century professors of anthropology and eighteenth-century Hawaiians or Englishmen. So it can be in any sociological enquiry, as much within a single society as between one society and another, or between the same society then and now. Sociologists can and do make mistakes about the roles of fellow-members of their own society no less than about those remote from them. Sometimes, indeed, an observer from a different society will do a better job than a native one. No American sociologist has ever written as perceptively about American society as did the Frenchman Alexis de Tocqueville, whose *Democracy in America*, published in 1835, remains to this day an inexhaustibly valuable source of insights into American modes of behaviour and thought. No better account of the state of English society at the end of the Napoleonic wars has been written than by the French historian Elie Halévy, whose *England in 1815* was published in 1912. For a sociologist to be a fellow-member of the same group, community, institution or society as he or she has chosen to study is neither a necessary nor a sufficient condition of getting it right. What matters is, as in all branches of science, whether the conclusions which the reader is invited to accept can be checked by, and with, other observers of evidence which is there for all to see.

Besides, there's no point in exaggerating the difficulties. There is no society anywhere in the world whose members' behaviour is literally incomprehensible to the members of another. You can read writings by philosophers, including Wittgenstein himself, in which they devise imaginary examples of peculiar people who appear to attribute meaning to propositions which violate any rules of meaning known to 'us'. In an article by the British philosopher

John Skorupski, the reader is asked to imagine a society whose members believe that the drawing-pins which they carry about with them in matchboxes are identical with the Empire State Building.[7] But no anthropologist has ever come back from anywhere in the world having found people who believe any such thing, any more than any anthropologist has ever found a people whose language proved impossible to learn. It may be difficult to establish *exactly* what meaning they attach to certain of their beliefs and the concepts in which they are expressed. But so it is back home. I have never read about an alien society whose religion struck me as any *more* bizarre than the Christian religion I was ostensibly reared in myself (Genesis, Incarnation, Resurrection, a God who is both Three and One, both Omnipotent and Benevolent, etc.). But I have no more difficulty in conducting meaningful social relationships with fellow-members of my own society who are serious, paid-up Christians than did the British anthropologist E. E. Evans-Pritchard with the Azande of the Northern Sudan, whose beliefs about magic, oracles and witchcraft were totally alien to him. Indeed, Evans-Pritchard is on record as saying that 'I found it strange at first to live among Azande and listen to native explanations of misfortunes which, to our minds, have apparent causes, but after a while I learned the idiom of their thought and applied notions of witchcraft as spontaneously as themselves in situations where the concept was relevant'; and what is more, 'I always kept a supply of poison for the use of my household and neighbours and we regulated our affairs in accordance with the oracles' decisions. I may remark that I found this as satisfactory a way of running my home and affairs as any other I know of.'[8]

So: however difficult it may be to establish what a fellow human being is 'really' thinking and therefore doing, it is always possible to identify not only the traits characteristic of an alien culture but the practices defining the roles by which institutions and societies remote in both time and place are constituted. There is, for example, no problem in equating the 'brothers-in-arms' whom we find swearing allegiance to each other in late medieval England[9] with the male *hetairoi* ('companions') who associated together with the same common objective of martial glory and lucrative plunder in archaic Greece many centuries earlier and miles away: in status-conscious, warlike, agrarian societies, young men without land of their own or a powerful patron have an evident incentive to join together in this way, whatever may be the other differences in both their cultural and their social environment. Likewise, when the French historian Fernand Braudel, in his magisterial study of the Mediterranean world in the sixteenth century, reports the way in which the Spaniards treated the fellow-members of their society who were of Muslim descent, he himself equates it with the treatment of blacks by poor whites in the southern states of America; and there is no difficulty in identifying cases from a wide range of places and times where a dominant ethnic or religious group discriminates against a subordinate one in the same immediately recognizable way.[10]

No less easy to find are cases where the same pattern of social behaviour can be observed in two different societies but with a difference in the function which it performs in each. If you look at ancient Roman society during its expansion by conquest in the first and second centuries BC, you will find free men fighting in the legions and slaves cultivating the large agricultural estates; but if you look at some no less warlike Islamic societies of the Middle East a few centuries later, you will find free men cultivating the land and armies made up of slaves. This, admittedly, gives scope for some unproductive argument over the precise definition of 'slavery'. Is the role of a slave soldier in an Islamic infantry regiment 'really' to be equated with that of a purchased chattel-slave in a Roman chain-gang? But, as always with such comparisons, the answer is not to quibble about the terms but to look at the practices which define the role. When you do – and the evidence is, in this instance, both abundant and reliable enough for the purpose – you will find that the institutional rules are such as in both cases to deny unequivocally to the 'slave' the power over his own person which attaches to the roles of the men who are institutionally defined as 'free'. And from comparisons like these there emerges the distinction, as important in sociology as in biology, between homologues (similarities of form) and analogues (similarities of function). The Roman slave is the homologue of the Islamic soldier and the analogue of the Islamic cultivator; the Islamic slave is the homologue of the Roman cultivator and the analogue of the Roman soldier. If this prompts you to ask: but what about combining the functions in a single role?, the answer is: yes, there are some of those too. In societies as far apart in time and place as seventh-century T'ang China, medieval Saxony, fourteenth-century Prussia under the 'Teutonic Knights', seventeenth-century Sweden, and eighteenth-century Russia you will find 'farmer-soldier' roles, in which the practices of smallholding and militia service were combined. And this illustrates another point common to biological and sociological theory: evolution can come about through *re-combination*, as well as mutation, of the units of selection.

Anyone observing a human society, including the observer's own, will not only be curious about some more than other aspects of the social behaviour of its members, but curious about one *level* of social behaviour rather than another. If you have chosen to study work-groups in a factory, or schoolchildren in a classroom, or doctors and their patients in a hospital you will be engaging in a different sort of project from what you will be doing if you want to study a society's institutions as such – its economy, or its type of government, or its form of organized religion. But not totally different. You can't study groups, however small, without taking account of the institutional context of the behaviour you are study-ing, and you can't study institutions, however large, without taking account of the behaviour of individual incumbents of specific roles.

The leading British sociologist David Lockwood pointed out in an influential article published in 1964 that 'system' integration – i.e., stability in the relations between institutions – is quite different from 'social' integration – i.e., stability in the relations between groups.[11] You may very well find that in the society you are studying there is much more of one than of the other: in societies as far apart as, for example, nineteenth-century Haiti and Egypt under the Mamluks, consistently high levels of inter-group hostility and violence were maintained within a largely unchanged set of economic, ideological and political institutions.[12] But you can't prise the two apart. You are always looking at the behaviour of people *in roles*; and there is not, and never will be, a society in which it is impossible to identify those roles or to trace their relations to each other at both the group and the institutional level.

Once, however, you have identified the society's constituent roles, you may want to proceed in either of two very different directions. You may, on the one hand, want to go on to ask 'why are these roles as they are?' (a question which itself, as we shall see in a moment, can be interpreted in several different ways). Or you may, on the other hand, want to ask 'what is it *like* to be one of the people occupying and performing one of these roles?' This second question, obviously, is one which doesn't arise at all in physics or chemistry. Not that it only arises in the study of the behaviour of human beings: some of the most remarkable recent research into the social behaviour of primates is directed precisely to establishing how far they do or don't attribute to each other minds like their own.[13] But this book is about the social behaviour of humans, and therefore organisms with minds which have the inborn capacity for all the richness and subtlety of language as spoken only by us. And it is this which gives the question 'what is it like to be a whatever-you-are?' not only its perennial interest but also its peculiar difficulties.

Unconvinced readers, fresh perhaps from 'postmodernist' texts, may protest that since I have already conceded the difficulty of establishing beyond argument what somebody else is 'really' thinking, I am hardly entitled to claim that even the most experienced sociologist can ever test an account of what is going on inside other people's heads in the way that an explanatory hypothesis about the externally visible influences on other people's externally visible behaviour can be tested if the requisite evidence is there. But there are two answers to this. First, the way to test a description of someone else's subjective experience is to try it out *on that person*; unless that person is deliberately seeking to mislead, as one or more of those teenage Samoan girls appear to have deliberately deceived the gullible Margaret Mead, the observer's description can be progressively expanded and refined to accord with what the person is willing to confirm as authentic. Second, in explanation just as much as in description, there comes a point at which, to borrow a metaphor from Wittgenstein, the spade is turned; children quickly discover that if they respond to every answer to a question 'why?' with another 'why?', the adult interlocutor is soon helpless. No sociologist – or psychologist – claims to be able literally to recreate the mental state of one person inside the mind of another. No heterosexual lover who has ever interrogated a partner about exactly what it feels like at the moment of orgasm will need to be told that empathy has a limit. But it would be absurd to conclude that different people can convey nothing to each other about the nature of their different subjective experiences. Indeed, it is sometimes the very incommensurability of subjective experience which can be deployed to good rhetorical effect. If a friend who has recently been bereaved says to you, 'My sense of desolation was more all-consumingly painful than you can possibly imagine', this may help you to understand the experience – understand it, that is, in the empathic, descriptive sense – better than any other words your friend might have chosen instead.

But however conducted, the exercise is a quite different one from the formulation of an explanatory hypothesis with which to account for the behaviour in question. It not only employs different techniques, but appeals to different standards, is open to different criticisms, and follows different rules. What's more, the description of a pattern of social behaviour as experienced by those whose behaviour it is may be not only at variance from, but in flat contradiction with, the hypothesis which turns out to explain it correctly. Nor is there anything to be surprised at in this, since, as any psychologist will tell you, all of us are likely to be mistaken about the causes of our own behaviour. Not totally, perhaps, and not always. But often enough for the disjunction between why we do what we do and what it is like for us to do it to be as important a feature of our social lives as any of the large-scale crises and upheavals for which sociologists studying our behaviour may be lying in wait at the institutional or societal level.

Descriptions of subjective experience, particularly at the cultural level, have traditionally been the domain of anthropologists rather than sociologists. But the division of labour between the two is largely conventional. Anthropologists tend to study alien cultures by living in them for a year or two and then reporting to their uninitiated compatriots on the curious habits and customs of the Azande, !Kung San, Eskimos, Hopi Indians, or whoever it may be. Nothing prevents them from doing the same back home. You can do fieldwork in Totnes as well as Tahiti. But as the range of such studies has broadened and their methods been refined, so has there increased the volume of debate on the same dilemma as arises from the travels of Herodotus or the arrival in Hawaii of Captain Cook. 'They' see the world very differently from the way in which 'we' do, and believe very different things about it. So what are the right terms for 'us' to use in describing 'them'? Ours or theirs?

If the question is put that way, the answer has to be 'theirs'. But it's a mistake to put it that way. It's true that anyone studying a society remote in either place or time from their own is likely to have to grasp ideas and beliefs very different from the culture in which they themselves were reared. But the measure of their success is precisely their ability to translate them back, as Evans-Pritchard and many other anthropologists have done, into terms comprehensible to 'us'; and the fact that it *can* be done is a conclusive demonstration that 'we' and 'they' are both variants of that same universal human nature acknowledged by Herodotus within which we and they are neither more nor less peculiar than each other. When, therefore, the American anthropologist Clifford Geertz enjoins his fellow-anthropologists in a much-quoted article to 'hawk the anomalous' and 'peddle the strange',[14] he is denying the very presupposition which legitimates his own professional practice. Who's more exotic, Professor? You or them? What makes those Balinese cockfights you're telling us about[15] any more anomalous or strange than those baseball games at the Yankee Stadium? And while you're about it, perhaps you can help us to understand an anomalous society like yours in which the topmost political role can be occupied by a former Grade B movie actor of limited intelligence called 'Ron' whose schedule is arranged for him by his wife under the guidance of an astrologer, and a strange culture like yours whose inherited complex of myths and symbols includes a pervasive totemic cult of an anthropomorphized duck called 'Donald' and an anthropomorphized mouse called 'Mickey'.

Geertz's article is called 'Anti-anti-relativism' because his perfectly legitimate concern is to emphasize how very different from one another different cultures and societies are. But the title is a pity all the same since relativism is a problem in philosophy – or, more strictly, in epistemology – rather than anthropology and sociology. The reason is simple. Any practising anthropologist or sociologist who takes epistemological relativism seriously has no option but to quit work. It's one thing to recognize that 'our' beliefs and values are not inherently privileged over 'theirs', but quite another to conclude that 'we' can therefore never make mean-ingful judgements of any kind about 'them'. What's the point of going out to do fieldwork among either the Balinese or the North Americans if all you're going to be able to come back with is an arbitrary description in untranslatable terms of their unreachable ideas about their illusory culture? If there is any pay-off from 'anti-anti-relativism', it is that it re-emphasizes the precept that since the results of anthropological, as of any other, research are a function not only of the evidence but of the assumptions with which the researcher approaches it, you had better be careful not to take your assumptions for granted. The dictum that 'the point of view creates the object' – which it does in natural and social science alike – may not have much immediate impact on the research of, say, a demographer who just wants to know by how much the Chinese birth-rate is going up or down or a political scientist who just wants to know how many female American voters have voted for one presidential candidate rather than another. It's obviously more relevant where the research is of the kind which can be vitiated by the unexamined assumptions of observers like those white men who didn't think to ask the Ashanti about the role of their Queen Mother. But to point that out is not to under-mine the status of anthropology as a serious academic discipline. On the contrary: it's all part of encouraging the next generation of anthropologists to get the cultures they choose to study more nearly right.

What, then, is the difference between getting it right in the explanatory ('why?') and the descriptive ('what is it like?') sense? Imagine yourself first to be a sociologist or anthropologist, whether in Totnes or Tahiti, trying to clinch the validity of a powerful-seeming explanatory hypothesis about 'their' behaviour which has dawned on you, and then to be the same sociologist or anthropolo-gist trying to make sure that a convincing-looking description of it which you have put together from your field-notes is truly authentic. As the first, you will be looking, ideally, for a decisive piece of evidence – an artefact, a document, a set of statistics, an observed pattern or sequence of behaviour – which will rule out alternative explanations but accord with your own. But as the second, you will be collecting a whole range of ancillary observations which will cumulatively reinforce the impression of 'what it was like' which you want to convey to your readers. If one of Professor Geertz's students were to say to him, 'I've read your article, but I still can't imagine taking cockfights as seriously as the Balinese do', Geertz's best tactic would be to load the student up with further details, other firsthand accounts, apposite metaphors or similies, and parallels from the student's own culture – including, perhaps, a baseball game at the Yankee Stadium – until the message finally gets home.

There's another revealing symptom of the difference, too. Explanation typically involves spotting a presumptively causal connection – without agriculture no feudalism, or whenever capitalism then democracy, or the Second World War because previously the First World War. But description typically involves what Wittgenstein calls 'seeing as'.[16] I cited Wittgenstein earlier as a philosopher whose fanciful examples of social behaviour, useful as they may be to philosophers concerned with the meaning of meaning, are useless if not positively misleading for practising sociologists or anthropologists. But on the mental process of 'seeing as', as he expounds it in his *Philosophical Investigations*, what he has to say is directly to the point. As an example (mine, not his), imagine yourself looking at a bulky, upright Remington typewriter of about the year 1900, and trying to see it as it would have been seen in the year in which it was made – as, that is, a piece of exciting, novel, up-to-the-minute, state-of-the-art technology. Can you do it? Try as I may, I'm not sure that I can. But the imaginative exercise required is the same as when an anthropologist tries to see a totem pole or a rain dance or an animal sacrifice or a Disney cartoon as 'they' see them. You don't do it by tracing the sequence of causes and effects which has made the objects of your curiosity what they are. You do it by bringing to bear your knowledge of the cultural context in which they occur and the language employed by the native informants whom you have interrogated about their significance to 'them'. And, once again, it's no different for a Balinese anthropologist trying to understand (in the emphatic, descriptive, 'what-is-it-like?' sense) a baseball game at the Yankee Stadium than for Professor Geertz trying to understand a Balinese cockfight.

Suppose, however, that seeing things as 'they' see them entails acceptance of beliefs which 'we' know to be false (or at any rate *think* we know to be false – the point stands even if we later decide that we were wrong). Let's go back to Evans-Pritchard among the Azande. He finds it quite easy to behave *as if* he shared their beliefs. But he can't and therefore doesn't actually share them, and he therefore can't, whatever further enquiries he makes, see the poison oracle as they do, any more than I can see the wafer in the hand of the Catholic priest as the body of Christ. Does it matter? No, it doesn't – not for the purposes of sociology. We don't have to *share* their beliefs in order to grasp their meaning to them and convey it to you, our readers. You don't, I assume, share any more than Herodotus did the belief of his Scythian informants that every member of the Neurian tribe is a once-a-year werewolf. But you can still grasp the concept (and enjoy the movie, too, if you don't find it too scary). Indeed, think what would happen if sociologists and anthropologists *did* all come to share the beliefs of the people whose patterns of behaviour they had been studying. They could only explain the behaviour correctly if the correct explanation had already been arrived at by those whose behaviour it was. And how often would that be?

What's more, this applies as much if not more when the beliefs in question are those of rulers, activists and decision-makers as when they are those of sociology professors. Rulers, activists and decision-makers all have explanations of their own of why the societies to which they belong are as they are as well as prescriptions of their own about how their societies ought to be changed for what they consider to be the better. But their memoirs are notorious for their unreliability. Only the most unsophisticated reader will be any more disposed to take them at face value than Evans-Pritchard to agree with his Zande informants that their misfortunes are due to the fact that one or more of their neighbours is a witch. But as you read the selective and tendentious reminiscences of important people, from Julius Caesar and before to Winston Churchill and since, and contrast them in your mind with the accounts of the same events given by uninvolved observers who have sought to test alternative possible explanations against one another, don't you at the same time find the disjunction between the two entirely comprehensible? As a species, we are not only a compulsively social but a compulsively self-justifying animal, and the autobiographies of politicians need to be checked for their veracity and lack of misleading insinuations and omissions no less carefully than those of philosophers do (Bertrand Russell's is a classic in this regard).[17] But the disjunction between what it felt like to the autobiographer at the time, and how it is going to be explained by revisionist professors fifty years after the autobiographer's death, is not a reason to question that that *was* what it felt like. The sociologist studying the societies in which the Great and Good (or Bad) occupied and performed their political roles may be as curious about the one as about the other, and increasingly struck by the irony inherent in the discrepancy between the two. But the discrepancy doesn't of itself make it any more difficult to arrive at an authentic description or a valid explanation – or both. On the contrary, understanding the delusions of grandeur that led to the downfall of Croesus or Louis Napoleon or Margaret Thatcher may make the causes of it all the easier to see.

*　　　*　　　*

But explanation, in sociology or elsewhere, can mean several different things. Why, to go back to my earlier example, do I shake hands with you when I'm introduced to you? Because I don't wish to seem impolite, because that's how I was brought up, because it strengthens social ties within our community, because a mutual friend decided that we should meet, because in our culture that's what we do instead of rubbing noses, or because in ruder and more violent times the symbolic meaning of a handshake was that neither of us held weapons in our hands?

That isn't even an exhaustive list. But for the practising sociologist the important distinction is the threefold one between *genetic, motivational* and *functional* explanations. This difference does not, let me emphasize, correspond to the difference between evoked, acquired and imposed behaviour: explanations of each kind can be sought for all three. But sociologists are, typically, more likely both to be studying imposed behaviour and to be looking for functional explanations. Let me go back once more to the example of infantry drill in seventeenth-century Europe. If you want to know where it came from, the answer lies in a narrative account of the development by Maurice of Nassau, captain-general of Holland and Zeeland for forty years from 1585, of systematic routines for marching and countermarching, loading and discharging matchlock guns, and transmitting words of command down through co-ordinated tactical units. If you want to know what influenced the people involved, the answer lies in the careers and ambitions of the leaders of early modern European armies on the one side and the dispositions and responses of volunteer or conscripted foot-soldiers on the other – responses which may, as I've pointed out already, be explained as much by an unconscious bonding effect of co-ordinated movement to the sound of drums or music as by a cultural process of deliberate imitation or learning. But if you want to know why it came to transform the way in which wars were fought, the answer lies in the competitive advantage which armies so drilled enjoyed over their opponents and the function which drill performed in promoting discipline during training and garrison duty as well as on the field of battle.

The same distinction can be made on topics which fall more nearly within the domain of one of the specialized social sciences. If, for example, you are an economist studying the automobile industry, you may want to know about the initial commercial exploitation of the internal combustion engine, in which case you will need to find out about the cost–benefit calculations which showed it to be worthwhile. Or you may want to know about the appeal of the product to its potential purchasers, in which case you will need to find out about not only its utility as a mode of transport but also the effect of advertising in expanding consumer demand for it and the part played by peer-group imitation or rivalry in raising its priority as an item of household expenditure. Or you may want to know why some manufacturers have been more successful than others, in which case you will need to find out about production techniques, marketing strategies, tariff barriers, and rates of technological innovation and obsolescence. Indeed, you may well want to draw directly on models derived from the theory of natural selection, as a number of economists have done, in order to explain why some particular firms and their particular products win out over others in competition for market share.[18]

These examples can also be used (as the handshake example can) to illustrate the difference between the approaches of sociologists or anthropologists on the one hand and historians on the other. There is a familiar contrast, much discussed by philosophers of social science, between narrative explanations ('because he couldn't find a horse, the King of Ruritania lost the battle and therefore his kingdom') and lawlike explanations ('all monarchies, including the Ruritanian, depend on some kind of religious legitimation'). But the contrast mustn't be overdrawn. Narrative explanations presuppose underlying regularities of certain kinds which must be true if the particular chain of causal connections is to hold; lawlike explanations are valid across the range of instances to which they are applied only if specific historical conditions are presupposed too. Lack of a horse only leads to the loss of a kingdom in a context to which implicit generalizations about certain forms of warfare apply, just as religious legitimation of a monarchy can only come about after a series of events which were contingently sufficient for it to do so. Sociologists, it could accordingly be said, are all closet historians (and historians closet sociologists).

For example: Madagascar is an exceptionally interesting area to study, not only because it is an island but because, over the course of the past 200 years, a network of small, scattered kingdoms has been replaced, first, by a central bureaucratic state employing slave labour, second, by a colonial regime which abolished slavery at the same time as imposing its own political institutions, and third, by a post-colonial government serviced by a professional, administrative and commercial bourgeoisie. This intriguing evolutionary pattern, convincingly analysed in the work of the anthropologist Maurice Bloch, presents a wide range of different contrasts which call for a correspondingly wide range of explanatory hypotheses. But if your interest is in the first of the three transitions, you will find yourself drawn to the particular sequence of events whereby a particular nineteenth-century king, having captured a sufficient number of slaves to exploit to the full the rice-growing potential of a particular territory, was able to exchange the surplus for European weapons which had by then become available and with them to capture yet more slaves and thereby build up a momentum of conquest which put his kingdom in control of the whole of Madagascar.[19] This is not only a textbook example of a narrative explanation; it also tells specifically against a would-be lawlike one since any generalization of the form of 'whenever one of a number of competing states gains priority of access to more advanced military technology it will establish a momentum of conquest sufficient to guarantee victory' can be demolished by counter-examples from other times and places where the other conditions which were necessary in the case of Madagascar failed to obtain.

But suppose that your interest is not in the political history of Madagascar, but on the contrary in the patterns of traditional social behaviour which have persisted throughout the successive changes of regime. Bloch draws attention to the persistence of a ritual of circumcision in which the ceremony is performed and the traditional blessing given by a chosen 'elder'.[20] He holds that in Madagascar, as elsewhere, such rituals are a function of institutionalized inequality, and is therefore unsurprised that the role of the persons chosen as 'elders' under each successive regime should turn out to be constant not in its defining practices but in its rank: in the first period, the ceremony is performed by local kinship group elders; in the second, by royal administrators; in the third, by French colonial officials; and in the fourth, by prominent local capitalists. QED. Notice, however, that he is explicitly not processing a lawlike generalization of the form of 'the amount of ritual communication in a society varies with the social distance between its constituent roles'. What he says is that institutionalized inequality is what rituals like this one are *about*. To explain them, accordingly, involves an analysis of both the meaning of the ritual to the participants and the features of the history and culture of Madagascar which account for the successive replacement of one kind of 'elder' by another. And yes, there *is* a valid generalization which can be framed, if you want it, to the effect that people prefer their domestic ceremonies presided over by persons of higher rather than lower rank. Would any professor of anthropology be flattered to have his or her inaugural lecture chaired not, as advertised, by the university vice-chancellor in academic robes, but by a bare-footed freshman in an unwashed T-shirt?

All this, however, brings us back to the need for genetic, motivational *and* functional explanation in the study of human social behaviour. For example: in many different societies, there are communities and subcultures where the advantages of behaviour which the dominant ideology defines as 'criminal' outweigh the disadvantages. Parts of London and Newcastle, as of Chicago and Los Angeles, are obvious examples. Able-bodied young males are likely to be at least part-time occupants and performers of the role of 'thief': the chances of being caught are small, there is no alternative employment on offer which is both legitimate and gainful, there are easy pickings in the more affluent community down the road, and so on. Yes, but why exactly *do* they do it? Is it through rational choice, unthinking conformity to the peer-group, class or ethnic hatred, innate predisposition, an urge to escape from boredom, pathological greed, or what? However obvious the function, we still want to know why those who do it do and those who don't don't, and which of the relevant features of the environment would need to be changed for those who do not to want to any longer. It still isn't a question to be answered by taking their own account of why they do it at face value: if, for example, they say that they do it because they are driven to it by poverty, the street-wise sociologist will wait for evidence of their changing their thieving behaviour when they cease to be poor. But don't we still want to know what motivates them to do it as well as how they started and what they get out of it? Of course we do.

Ideally, therefore, the explanation of an observed pattern of human social behaviour will not only link a motivational to both a genetic and a functional hypothesis but provide a theoretical underpinning for all three. You don't need a sociology degree before you notice that young men are more aggressive than elderly women. But maybe you do need a sociology degree (with some biology and psychology courses thrown in) before you can produce an adequate answer to the question: why does what looks like a causal connection between young maleness and a propensity to violence hold good? We need not just the evidence which might, but doesn't, invalidate the claim that the connection *is* causal. We also need an explanation for the explanation. To take a textbook example from physical science, the discovery of a causal connection between altitude above sea level and the boiling point of water was made long before the notion of atmospheric pressure provided the theoretical grounding for it. In sociology, we are still a long way from the sort of grounding of wide-ranging causal hypotheses in deep and powerful theories which has been achieved in both physical and biological science. But that's part of what makes it such a fascinating subject to pursue. Whatever (exactly) it is that you want to know, there is plenty left to find out about how we all behave as social animals, and there are plenty of alternative hypotheses available to explain it when you do.

Then what, in all this, about the philosophers, preachers and poets? Don't they offer both explanations and descriptions of patterns of human social behaviour as valid and authentic as those put forward by academic social scientists? Well – nothing stops them. Nietzsche's writings, to take a celebrated example, contain a number of sociological conjectures about the evolution of human nature for which he himself claimed 'scientific' status, including his view of systems morality as expressions of sublimated feelings of resentment towards those with power on the part of those without it. But Nietzsche wasn't setting out systematically to test a set of explanatory hypotheses against the evidence most likely to conflict with them. He was, for his own very different purposes, constructing a just-so story about the 'genealogy of morals' and using it to subvert the conventional view of what human beings are doing in passing judgement on each other's behaviour at all. The writings of philosophers, preachers and poets *are* sociology to the extent that the authors make them so. Some of the most potent intellectual cocktails yet mixed, like Freud's, derive their potency precisely from the cunning, not to say dangerous, way in which they combine the two: would-be therapeutic regimes derived from a psychoanalytic theory which fails the standard tests to which new therapeutic drugs are routinely subjected may turn out to do more harm than good. But the difference between the kinds of conclusions to which the reader is asked to assent is still the same. It isn't up to you or me whether Sahlins or Obeyesekere is right about the Hawaiians' reception of Captain Cook, even though our respective ideological presuppositions may lead us to hope and expect that it's the one rather than the other. But we do have, and will continue to have, a further element of discretion in deciding whether or not we share Nietzsche's unflattering view of the Christian conception of morality, even after every item of relevant evidence is in.

To emphasize the difference as firmly as I have been doing is not – repeat not – to question that to analyse it is a philosophical rather than a scientific exercise: the philosophy of science is a branch of philosophy, not of science. So when the French philosopher and literary critic Jacques Derrida, in his book *On Grammatology*, announces to his readers that the nature of the difference between a philosophical and an empirical question isn't simply an empirical question, the (or at least, my) surprise is that he feels the need to italicize it.[21] Who is he contradicting? There is always scope for argument over the borderline. But no contemporary sociologist *or* philosopher holds that the conceptual distinction between conceptual and empirical questions is 'simply empirical'. Likewise, when textbooks on the philosophy of social science correctly insist that social scientists themselves are both its subjects and its objects, who wants to say otherwise? The question is: what follows? And the answer is that although social scientists are on that account exposed to the risk of making mistakes of a kind which doesn't arise at all in the study of inanimate nature, it doesn't prevent them from formulating explanatory hypotheses about their own and other people's behaviour which can be tested by the same criteria of validity. Empirical sociologists talking about facts and their causes are apt to be denounced by their more philosophically minded colleagues as 'positivists'. By this, the anti-positivists usually mean to imply a nefarious commitment to an ideology of science which denies the truism that the practice of science raises some genuinely philosophical issues. But when they come to attack the empiricists' specific conclusions, you can bet that they will tacitly acknowledge the existence of empirical criteria by which observations of, and hypotheses about, patterns of human social behaviour stand and fall. Or if they persist in maintaining that all 'social facts' are 'ideological constructions', you need merely ask them whether, if charged by a court of law with a murder committed by somebody else, they would accept that their innocence was *only* an ideological construction (which the concept of 'murder' as an act of intentional, wrongful killing self-evidently is), and not in any sense a 'fact'.

There is, to be sure, nothing self-contradictory in doing both. All students of human social behaviour, whatever label they attach to themselves, are free to draw on whatever empirical observations they like in order to persuade their readers to share their personal convictions about the human condition, the meaning of history, the phenomenology of the life-world, the postmodern experience, the contradictions of rationality, the dualism of knowledge and action, the existential dilemma, the ontology of social life, the paradox of reflexive subjectivity, and so on and so forth. The sociologists of the kind whom their opponents denounce as 'positivists' are apt to be no less contemptuous of those whom they in their turn denounce as practitioners of 'substitute religion'. But each is as legitimate an intellectual activity as the other. The two are not in competition except in the trivial sense that professors giving lectures of the one kind may be competing for student audiences with professors giving lectures of the other. One of the most influential contemporary practitioners of 'substitute religion' is the German philosopher Jürgen Habermas, whose ambition (if I understand him correctly) is to formulate the ideal conditions under which rational human beings could communicate with each other free of the constraints imposed by 'positivist' social theory and the social institutions which it reflects. It is, in my judgement, a heroic but ultimately self-defeating intellectual enterprise. But whether my judgement is right or wrong, it's an enterprise as fundamentally different as Nietzsche's is from seeking first to distinguish and then to explain the different patterns of human social behaviour to be found in the historical and ethnographic record and then, if the researcher is so minded, to describe what they have been like, subjectively speaking, for the people whose patterns of behaviour they are. The only kind of philosophical argument to which this book stands categorically opposed is one which seeks to deny that empirical sociology is possible at all. But that sort of argument is best countered simply by doing what the sceptic says can't be done; and, as I've hinted already, you will find even the most anti-positivist practitioners of substitute religion doing it too, where and when it bolsters their arguments of the other kind.

III

A Catalogue of Errors

IF SOCIOLOGY IS AS OLD as Herodotus and Aristotle – to say nothing of Herodotus's Chinese contemporary K'ung Fu Tzu, otherwise known as Confucius – you may well wonder why it has taken so long to get as far as it has. But the same could be said about many other branches of science. Although mankind's attempts to make sense of both the natural and the social world go back for many thousands of years, it's remarkable how recent is the dramatic increase in knowledge which has transformed the world and the way we live in it. How and why it has happened is itself a controversial question. But the fact remains that physics, chemistry, biology, psychology and sociology as they are now understood and practised are all a product of the past couple of centuries or less.

This isn't to say that earlier ideas about the workings of the social as well as the natural world were all mistaken. Aristotle had some good ones, not least about the relationship within a society between political stability and the relative size of its middle class – a hypothesis lent additional support as recently as 1996 by evidence set out in an article published in the *Journal of Economic Growth*.[1] So did the fourteenth-century Islamic political theorist Ibn Kaldun, who detected in the societies which he studied a recurrent tendency for them to oscillate between government by egalitarian warriors from the desert and hierarchical bureaucrats in the towns. So did Machiavelli, whose insights into the pursuit of power and the means of its retention by the rulers of the city-states of late Renaissance Italy have made his name a part of our everyday vocabulary. But all such ideas were, and were bound to be, relatively parochial in their scope and imprecise in their formulation by the standards of late twentieth-century sociology. The term 'sociology' was itself only coined in the nineteenth century by Auguste Comte, who to that extent has to be acknowledged as its founder. But Comte's writings, for all that he was remarkably prescient about the global impact of industrialization, are nowadays studied closely only by those whose interests lie on the wilder shores of defunct ideas. The sociologists who did most to make the subject into what it still, for the time being, is are Karl Marx, Max Weber and Emile Durkheim. It would, I think, be fair to say that there is no serious sociologist now writing who has been untouched by any trace of their influence. But there is something rather odd here. In all sciences the advances made in one generation are likely to be superseded in the next, usually through their absorption into a deeper or more wide-ranging theory. What is striking about these three founding fathers of sociology is how far they all went astray in their quest for the Big Idea.

With Marx, much of the difficulty (but at the same time, much of the reason for his influence) is his fusion of sociological with philosophical argument in precisely the way I had in mind in the concluding paragraphs of Chapter II. Literally thousands of books and articles have been written about the relationship between the 'scientific' and the 'humanistic' Marx. Nor is that surprising, given the enormous appeal of a doctrine combining a messianic prophecy of a better world with a hypothesis both supporting the prophecy and at the same time endorsing a revolutionary programme to make it come true. But he didn't get it right. Marx's belief that the course of human history is determined by conflict between a dominant class and a subordinate class which in due course replaces it led him to predict that the 'proletariat' would shortly displace the 'bourgeoisie' and usher in a utopian social order about

47

whose details he was notoriously vague. But as a Polish joke was later to put it, 'Under capitalism man exploits man; under socialism it's the other way round.' Marx's sociology was mistaken in three ways. First, he was wrong in supposing that in capitalist industrial societies the progressive immiseration of an expanding proletariat would lead to a revolutionary transfer of power. Second, he was wrong in supposing that where socialist revolutions did come about, they would do so in industrial rather than still predominantly agricultural societies. Third, he was wrong in supposing that in socialist societies class conflict would come to an end. So why, you may well ask, is he still taken so seriously? The short answer is that he has made it impossible for any subsequent sociologist to look at the world and the human societies in it without conceding a more prominent part to class conflict and what he called the 'social relations of production' than had been admitted in pre-Marxist sociology. In that sense, and to that extent, 'we are all Marxists now'.

Max Weber, who was born nearly half a century after Marx, disagreed with the Marxists not because he didn't recognize the importance of class conflict in human history but because he denied that all other forms of conflict could be reduced to it. Not only did he see political as opposed to economic interests as having their own independent part to play, but he also gave to ideas, and particularly religious ideas, an importance which the Marxists denied them. Ideas, as he put it in a memorable phrase, are like switchmen diverting the course of history down one railway track rather than another.[2] His own view of history was as a process of inexorable 'rationalization' originating in the societies of early modern Europe. But, like Marx, he turns out not to have got it right. Whatever he meant by 'rationalization', it is not the inexorable process which he supposed – even though he saw it as being interrupted by the occasional emergence of a 'charismatic' religious or political leader – and it is not to Europe alone that the modern advance of science and technology is due. Yet Weber, too, has permanently influenced his successors. The best way for me to convey this is not to try and summarize his most enduring contributions, but simply to point out how often I mention him in this book. The eminent French sociologist Raymond Aron once said that Weber is not merely the greatest sociologist but *the* sociologist,[3] and it is hard to think of any other for whom the claim could plausibly be made.

And Durkheim? Durkheim was a near-contemporary of Weber's (although, to the puzzlement of later historians of ideas, they never took any account of each other's work). Unlike Weber, however, Durkheim sought to establish sociology as an autonomous subject by postulating a conceptual realm of the 'social' in which human institutions were all to be explained by reference to other 'social facts', these being defined as such by the 'collective consciousness' of the society in question. This extrapolation from the unquestionably valid observation that social behaviour is not simply a matter of individual choice has proved seductive to more anthropologists than sociologists, perhaps because of their stronger sense of the importance in human societies of custom and ritual. But it is flawed for a reason which Durkheim seems never to have grasped. If human social behaviour is explicable entirely by the social environment within which the persons whose behaviour it is have been brought up, then this must include the way they conceptualize their behaviour to themselves – an inference which Durkheim was, in fact, explicitly willing to draw. But the inference rests on a fallacy. For if, as Durkheim believed, even the concept of duality derives from a perception of dualities in the social organization of society, how can they be perceived to *be* dualities without some innate prior capacity for doing so? Quite apart from the findings of evolutionary psychology and biological anthropology, which have undermined the conception of the human mind as a blank slate on which society imprints what it may, there is a logical error here reminiscent of the old chestnut about the painter El Greco being astigmatic (work it out for yourself if you don't know the answer already). In Durkheim's last book, he went so far as to argue, by a sort of reverse-evolutionary study of the Australian Arunta, that all religion is essentially the worship of society by itself – as if much religious doctrine and practice weren't explicitly hostile to the established institutions of the societies in which they have arisen on that very account. As Evans-Pritchard later remarked, it was Durkheim, not the 'savage', who turned Society into a God.[4]

And yet, and yet. We are all to some degree Durkheimians now, just as we are all to some degree Weberians and Marxists. It's not just that so many of Durkheim's preoccupations are ours too: the division of labour in complex industrial societies, the psychological stress produced by social disequilibrium, the importance of associations intermediate between the individual and the state, or the relation between public education and private morality. It's also that there *is* a sense in which societies and cultures are more than the sum of their members' behaviour, and their members *do* tacitly acknowledge this in much of what they say and do. Look at how people participate in rituals of various kinds even when they are indifferent to the ideology purporting to legitimate them, or how they respond collectively and seemingly unthinkingly to patriotic symbols, or how they conform to social changes which are not of their own making. The correct explanation of these patterns of behaviour may be different from what Durkheim supposed. But he was right to see them as incompatible with the dogmatically individualist assumptions which he attributed to earlier economic and political theorists, the British 'Utilitarians' included. If, like Comte before him, he was to prove mistaken in undervaluing individual psychology, it doesn't follow that he was wrong to deny that sociology is nothing more than individual psychology writ large.

Ironically, neither Marx nor Weber nor Durkheim were as

influential in their lifetimes as the self-educated Victorian railway engineer Herbert Spencer; and since it was Spencer who actually coined the unfortunate phrase 'survival of the fittest', you may well wonder why I have left him off my list. But Spencer's sociology was more irreparably flawed than Marx's, Weber's or Durkheim's by his conception of evolution as a cosmic process of mechanistic advance towards a harmonious equilibrium and his simultaneous conviction that a scientific ethics could be derived from the laws of a uniform Nature. To be sure, for Marx class conflict was to lead to an eventual state of universal harmony, just as for Spencer individual competition was to do so. But Spencer's appeal to his contemporaries, particularly in the United States,[5] derived less from the conviction carried by his account of universal human history than from the ostensibly scientific legitimation which he gave to unfettered competition in pursuit of personal gain. He was, of course, perfectly right to point out how strenuously individuals do compete with one another for personal gain (and not by any means only in the United States). But he failed to see how little that actually explains about why a given society's economic, ideological and political institutions come to be what they are.

With hindsight, it's unsurprising that the nineteenth-century conception of social evolution survived into the twentieth century in its Marxian rather than its Spencerian form. It did so not only because of the increasing attraction of Marxism as a reasoned prophecy of the overthrow of capitalism, but also because of the steadily diminishing attraction of Spencer's refusal to countenance the involvement of the state in matters of social welfare. Not that Spencer fell out of favour entirely. He even enjoyed something of a revival in the 1960s, and the American sociologist Talcott Parsons, who in 1937 had opened his first book, *The Structure of Social Action*, by quoting from the historian Crane Brinton the rhetorical question 'Who now reads Spencer?', can be found in 1966 publishing a little book called *Societies* in which he explicitly readmits into sociology the notion of evolution in terms which could have been written by Spencer himself (complete with the mistake of equating evolution with progress).[6] But Marxism aside, the dominant ideas in twentieth-century sociology have been explicitly anti-evolutionary. There are three of them: Functionalism, Structuralism and Behaviorism (deliberately spelled without the 'u' – it's very much an American doctrine).

Functionalism was most influentially expounded in the 1920s by the anthropologists Bronislaw Malinowksi and A. R. Radcliffe-Brown – the latter explicitly influenced by Durkheim. Its basic tenet was that the distinctive patterns of behaviour observable in different human societies are to be explained not in terms of their history but in terms of the contribution which the behaviour makes to the workings of the society as a whole. As a reaction against the purely conjectural histories to which many nineteenth-century evolutionists had committed themselves, this was salutary. But it invited the obvious rejoinder that change has still to be explained. After all, even the stablest-looking societies were different at some time in the past and will be different again at some time in the future. To this, the functionalist reply is that when a society *does* change, the explanation of what it changes into will still depend on an analysis of the function of the new institutions which have emerged in place of the old. But the flaw which remains is the implicit presupposition that the normal state of human societies is an equilibrium between their component parts. No theory which purports to be able to explain why human societies are as we find them can possibly dispense with the notion of function. But nor can it achieve its intended purpose if it fails to acknowledge that conflict and change are as 'normal' a feature of human societies as cohesion and stability. It's not just that the explanation of change requires an analysis of the functions of the practices by which the society's roles are defined rather than of the connections between the institutions constituted by them. It's also that those mutant practices which turn out to be the critical ones may do so precisely because the advantage which they confer on the roles that carry them is *mal*adaptive for the society's institutions and thereby for the society itself in its relations with other societies.

Similarly Structuralism, of which the French anthropologist Claude Lévi-Strauss is perhaps the most celebrated practitioner, by likewise downplaying the value of historical explanation furnished a salutary reminder of the importance of studying the form as well as the content of patterns of human behaviour. But again, it depends what (exactly) you want to know. Of all the social sciences, linguistics is the one where structuralist explanations have been most illuminating. But even at a less profound level than the famous American linguist Noam Chomsky's analysis of syntactic structure and grammatical transformation rules, it's easy to show how a previously puzzling system of terminology can be accounted for in purely structural terms. As the British anthropologist Edmund Leach put it in the case of the highly complex kinship terminology of a people called the Jinghpaw, structural analysis shows it to be 'the simplest possible logical system consistent with the rules of the society'.[7] But even if this is correct, can the genetic and motivational questions be entirely ignored? To show that a piece of music is a fugue tells us nothing about either the composer's motive in writing it or the antecedent cultural and social conditions without which it would never have been composed at all. The demonstration by Chomsky and his followers that there is a universal grammar innate to the human species which underlies all the particular grammars of the enormous number of different human languages still leaves it to be shown where and how language evolved in the first place, how linguistic competence relates to other mental abilities, and whether gestural rather than verbal communication may hold the key to the origin of language. The search for what the French philosopher Maurice

Merleau-Ponty called 'the programme of a universal code of structures, which would allow us to deduce them from one another by means of transformation-rules' cannot, whatever else it may achieve, lead to a general theory of how human cultures and societies function and evolve.[8]

The self-defeating consequence of trying to banish rather than incorporate alternative approaches is more apparent still with Behaviorism. Its founder was the American psychologist John B. Watson, who proclaimed in a much-quoted passage first published in 1925 that given what he called 'my own specified world to bring them up in' he could train any set of randomly chosen healthy infants to grow up to be 'any type of specialist I might select – doctor, lawyer, artist, merchant-chief, and yes, even beggarman and thief.'[9] Quite a claim! Notice, however, that it is the mirror-image of Durkheim's notion that it is Society which makes us all into what we are. Both claims presuppose that human beings as they emerge from the womb are completely malleable: the difference is that Watson thinks of individuals as being moulded by other individuals whereas Durkheim thinks of them as being moulded by the collective consciousness of Society itself. This has the advantage for Behaviorists that, unlike Durkheimians, they can't be accused of invoking what the American philosopher Daniel C. Dennett disparagingly calls 'skyhooks' – that is, imaginary ' "mind-first" powers or processes' to which causal agency is attributed in some arbitrary and untestable way.[10] What's more, it enables Behaviorists to devise experiments in which, by the judicious manipulation of rewards and punishments, human beings and animals alike can be made to behave differently than they otherwise would. But as a general theory of human behaviour, Behaviorism falls flat on its face. It treats the brain as a 'black box' whose content is immaterial: B. F. Skinner, the most influential Behaviorist of the generation after Watson, resolutely dismissed as unscientific 'mentalism' any suggestion that the internal state of the person whose behaviour is being studied has anything to contribute to establishing the causal link between the stimulus of what the Behaviorists call 'operant conditioning' and the response manifested in the outward and visible actions of the experimental subject. (There are, as you might expect, lots of good Behaviorist jokes, of which my favourite is that when two of them meet in the street each says to the other: 'You're fine. How am I?') To insist, however, that what is going on in the subject's mind (or brain) *is* relevant to explaining the subject's behaviour needn't involve recourse to one of Dennett's phantasmagorical 'skyhooks'. The most powerful single body-blow to Behaviorism was delivered by Chomsky in 1959 in a devastating review of Skinner's book *Verbal Behavior*.[11] Chomsky showed that language-learning cannot be accounted for in stimulus–response terms: there has to be an inborn capacity which enables children to construct entirely novel sentences which they can't possibly have learned by example and imitation. This was not enough by itself to win over the die-hards, including the distinguished American sociologist George C. Homans, Parsons's colleague at Harvard, who continued to believe that studies like his own of what he called the 'elementary forms' of human social behaviour must be grounded, theoretically speaking, in a recognizably Skinnerian model of individual responses to the stimuli of punishment or reward.[12] But the declining band of Skinnerians is by now virtually extinct. And it is a nice irony that Skinner so far exemplified in his own behaviour the power of 'operant conditioning' that he could never bring himself to read Chomsky's review.

It might seem tempting to suggest that the slogan to which all this leads is: Stamp Out All 'Isms'. But that would be much too sweeping, not least given what I've been saying myself about Darwinism. Since some explanatory theories stand up very much better than others to attempted refutation, there can't be much harm in encapsulating their distinctiveness in a word coined for the purpose. All the same, however, there are two good reasons to be very, very careful about doing so.

The first reason is that the theory risks becoming not a set of propositions held to be true but a set of doctrines held to be sacrosanct – or, to put it in terms which go back to Francis Bacon in the seventeenth century, that its adherents become less concerned to have their errors corrected than their doubts removed. Marxism is the obvious example, as recognized not least by sophisticated Marxists who are themselves at pains to assure their readers that despite the eschatological tinge to much of what Marx wrote, they do not subscribe to it as if to Holy Writ. Belief *in* something-or-other, as opposed to belief *that* something-or-other, is an attitude of mind very easy to understand. It is, after all, painful to subject deeply-held convictions to constant test; it is tempting to dismiss unwelcome criticism as made in bad faith; and it is reassuring to fall back on canonical authority. But that's not the attitude of mind best calculated to advance the cause of scientific discovery.

The second reason is that the theory in question risks being thought to account for a much wider range of observations than in fact it can. Behaviorism is, as I have already implied, the obvious example of this. However remarkable (and they were) Skinner's demonstrations that the responses of pigeons and rats to experimental stimuli were not only explicable but predictable in terms of 'operant conditioning', they didn't entitle him to claim that the same was bound to hold for behaviour in general. But that's just what promulgation of the term 'Behaviorism' inevitably does. It's as much to be expected that people who come up with good original ideas should claim too much for them as it is that their disciples should then elevate them into an inviolable orthodoxy. But again, that's not the most promising way to advance the cause of scientific discovery.

*   *   *

It would be agreeable to suppose that by correctly diagnosing the errors of sociologists of the past, sociologists of the present could be saved from making any of their own. Needless to say, however, that isn't how it works in sociology any more than anywhere else. Not only are there always new mistakes as well as new discoveries to be made, but discoveries can only be made by actually making them. Yet forewarned is, as they say, forearmed. There are two further dangers which aren't so much mistakes as misconceptions, and which account for much of the bad press which sociology receives. They are, moreover, dangers to which sociologists are unavoidably prone, partly because we are ourselves examples of what we are studying and partly because we have, in consequence, a disposition to overvalue our own opinions about ourselves. The first danger is to suppose that a favoured proposition about human social behaviour is new and true when it is merely new; the second is to suppose that a favoured proposition is new and true when it is merely true.

The sociologists whom I have in mind I propose to label AMs and PMs. The AMs are the Attitude-Merchants, those who allow their personal views about the behaviour they are studying to inform their conclusions about it to the point that they neglect or devalue uncomfortable evidence for the sake of those views. The PMs are the Platitude-Merchants, those who allow their conviction of the importance of some general truths about human behaviour to convince them that by rephrasing those truths in more impressive-sounding words – or, sometimes, more impressive-looking but nonetheless trivial mathematical equations – they are advancing sociological knowledge. (There are also the occasional BMs, or Beatitude-Merchants, of whom Jesus of Nazareth is the one whose teachings will probably be best known to older readers. But the Sermon on the Mount, although it may be very good religion, is very bad sociology: the meek may be blessed but they are not, whatever else, going to inherit the earth.)

The best-known PM in the literature of sociology is Talcott Parsons, whom we saw just now backing off from his earlier disparagement of Herbert Spencer towards a belated recognition that societies all do, after all, evolve from one kind into another. Homans, during his years with Parsons at Harvard, was always proclaiming that the emperor had no clothes, and justifying himself in doing so with the remark that he couldn't be accused of hitting a man when down. In the same spirit, let me come clean and say that I have agreed with Homans ever since I first heard Parsons lecture in the academic year 1958–9, and it has never ceased to surprise me that he should have been taken as seriously as he was – and by some sociologists, still is. One suggested explanation favoured by some of his commentators is that his elaborate terminology and claims to be expounding a comprehensive theory of social systems gave sociologists who hadn't been tempted by Marxism a gratifying sense of an alternative professional identity. A slightly different explanation, favoured by his critics who *have* been tempted by Marxism, is that his emphasis on the self-equilibrating interdependence of the constituent parts of social systems was deeply comforting to adherents of the American ideology of consensual liberalism. But whatever the explanation of his reputation, the question which his admirers have to address is: what did he discover, or alternatively refute, about human groups, communities, institutions or societies which was both original and profound? I have yet, after all these years, to hear a convincing answer. There is much in Parsons's voluminous writings which there is no cause to dispute because they are little more than common-sense observations about the institutions of American society. There is also much which there is no cause to dispute because it consists of general statements which are analytically true within his own conceptual scheme. There are also some useful comments about the writings of earlier sociologists, particularly Weber whose work Parsons did much to make better known to English-speaking readers.

But if there is a self-styled Parsonian out there who can produce for me a set of well-tested hypotheses grounded in Parsons's conceptual scheme by which previously accepted explanations of some important aspect of human social behaviour have been overthrown, I will, as the saying goes, eat my copy of *The Structure of Social Action* for breakfast.

Parsons is by no means alone among sociologists in being accused of empty verbiage and unnecessary jargon. But he has the distinction of having provoked the most memorably outspoken attack on 'grand theory' yet on record, by his fellow-American C. Wright Mills in a book called *The Sociological Imagination* published in 1959. Mills was the sort of sociologist whose critics are apt to dismiss him as an up-market journalist who doesn't have a theory at all beyond a generalized hostility to the established institutions of his own society. But his own two best-known books about the mid-twentieth century United States, *The Power Elite* and *White Collar*, are not necessarily the worse on that account. Anyway, his attack on Parsons, which includes a devastating four-paragraph 'translation' (Mills's word) of the 555 pages of Parsons's *The Social System*, should be copied out every morning by any sociologist who thinks that a platitude is less of a platitude if it's dressed up in more and longer words. Thus Parsons: 'Attachment to common values means, motivationally considered, that the actors have common "sentiments" in support of the value patterns, which may be defined as meaning that conformity with the relevant expectations is treated as a "good thing" relatively independently of any specific instrumental "advantage" to be gained from such conformity, e.g., in the avoidance of negative sanctions.' Which is rendered by Mills: 'When people share the same values, they tend to behave in accordance with the way they expect one another to behave.' Unfair? Only a little. To a recent defender of Parsons, Leon H. Mayhew, Mills is guilty of a 'wilful desire to misunderstand and distort'.[13] But to this reader, at least, Professor Mayhew's

'Introduction' to his selection of Parsons's writings does a lot more to confirm Mills's strictures than to rebut them. When, shortly after Mills's attack, the philosopher Max Black undertook a critical examination of Parsons's writings, he was driven to conclude that 'He has provided us with a web of concepts, whose correspondence with the concepts which laymen use for thinking about social relations and human action is barely disguised by a new terminology', and he ended with the outspoken confession, 'I have not concealed my dismay at the conceptual confusions that in my judgement pervade the entire structure.'[14]

But take care: you may find yourself rejecting a PM look-alike who turns out not to be one after all. Here is a quote which looks at first sight as emptily verbose as anything which Parsons ever wrote:

> The habitus, the durably installed generative principle of regulated improvisations, produces practices which tend to reproduce the regularities immanent in the objective conditions of the production of their generative principle, while adjusting to the demands inscribed as objective potentialities in the situation, as defined by the cognitive and motivating structures making up the habitus.[15]

A sentence like that is begging for the Wright Mills treatment, of which a possible version might be:

> The history of consistent behaviour within a social group, as well as its members' reactions to their immediate environment, is necessary to account for its distinctive forms of apparently spontaneous behaviour.

I may not have got that quite right, and to the extent that I haven't I apologize to Professor Pierre Bourdieu, from whose *Outline of a Theory of Practice* the sentence is taken. But that isn't the point. The point is that Bourdieu is saying something subtle and (I think) valid about the process by which practices are replicated within a group or wider community sharing a common culture. And if a sceptical reader wants to know what the pay-off is in the currency of science, the answer is that Bourdieu has, in addition to his literary and philosophical writings, done sociological research out of which have come convincing explanations of specific patterns of social behaviour including, for example, the transmission of 'cultural capital' in the French educational system and the spatial lay-out of the domestic apartments of the Kabyle of Algeria and its relation to the division of labour in Kabyle society between men and women. There is, accordingly, a twofold reason for wanting to show the PMs up for what they are. Not only do they make sociology seem more pretentiously trivial than it is, but they tar with their brush the writings of other sociologists whose genuine contributions to the explanation of human social behaviour thereby risk being dismissed as less illuminating than they are.

Much the same can be said about the Attitude-Merchants as about the Platitude-Merchants. Not only do they make sociology look indistinguishable from propaganda, but they encourage the readers of other sociologists to suspect us all of nursing more or less well hidden agendas of a political kind. In the spirit of Homans on Parsons, I have chosen as my example of a leading AM a sociologist whose position is such that I likewise can't be accused of kicking a man when down – Professor Immanuel Wallerstein, who at the time of writing is President of the International Socio-logical Association. Wallerstein's reputation derives from two influential volumes under the title *The Modern World-System*. Their argument, in summary, is that capitalism plays the role in a global context which Marxism assigned to it in a national context – in other words, weak peripheral nations, like subordinate classes, are exploited by stronger core nations whose strength is a function of economic rather than either ideological or political domination within the global market. Now there is much that is persuasive about this argument, and much of it has been incorporated into

61

the writings of other historians and sociologists who may or may not share all of his views. But Wallerstein *hates* capitalism. He hates it like a Sunni Muslim hates a Shiite Muslim, or a Freemason a Jesuit, or a Rangers supporter a Celtic one. And he is, of course, perfectly entitled to do so. But his attitude effectively blinds him to the possibility that capitalism explains less than he supposes about why one rather than another European society has at one time or another been more or less dominant within the 'world-system'. In particular, it leads him to ignore the other, political determinants of the remarkable rise of Sweden and Prussia, which cannot be fitted to his model as comfortably as he claims. It's not that he isn't aware of the problem. It's that he wants to blame capitalism for everything he dislikes, and the reality is more complicated than that.

There's nothing wrong with a bit of polemic. Haven't I just commended Chomsky for his attack on Skinner, and before that Weber for his resistance to Marx? The history of ideas is full of examples where an outstanding thinker is pushed to make a lasting contribution through hostility to the conventional wisdom, whether, like Kant, 'roused from his dogmatic slumbers' by the need to take issue with the scepticism of David Hume, or, like Keynes, driven to overturn the 'classical' economic theory in which he had been reared by its failure to account for persistent large-scale unemployment. The trouble about the Attitude-Merchants isn't that they hold their attitudes as strongly as they do. It's that they let their attitudes run away with them. And where those attitudes are shared by their readers, this compounds the risk that the explanations they advance of the behaviour about which they feel so strongly won't be tested against the evidence as rigorously as it should be or even tested at all.

I have by now lost count of the number of times over the past thirty years when I have been asked by a colleague in another academic field to answer the charge that sociology is a 'soft option', or 'not a real subject'. I know only too well what they mean. Even if the 'substitute religion' is moved, as it should be, to a separate wing of the University Library and a separate department within the Faculty of Arts and Sciences, too much of what passes for sociology can be charged with being neither science on the one hand nor scholarship on the other. Where (it is asked) is our Newton, or even our Copernicus, let alone our Einstein? Why do we devote so much time to discussing our methods instead of using our methods to arrive at conclusions both new and true about the institutions and societies in which we and others live? What does it say about our subject that its leading journals keep publishing articles about the 'state of the discipline', the 'crisis in sociology', and the fact that, as the American sociologist Randall Collins plaintively remarked in one such article in 1989, 'Much of what we express today about each other's work is negativistic, hostile, dismissive'?[16] But the conclusion to be drawn from comments of this kind is the opposite of what is implied by those who make them. Sociology may be easy to do badly (what isn't?). But the lesson of its history to date is how hard it is to do well. To sociologists, this should be a challenge rather than a deterrent. But to their readers, it should be a reason to be at the same time sceptical about sociology's pretensions, charitable about its limitations, and discriminating about its achievements. On that note, I shall do my best to tell you in the next few chapters a little of what we do and don't know about why the various human groups, communities, institutions and societies which there are and have been in the world are and have been as we find them.

IV

Power

THE CONCEPT OF POWER is so important in sociology that it needs a chapter to itself. Sociology is the study of people in their roles, and to study people in their roles is to study how and why power is distributed and exercised in the groups, communities, institutions and societies to which the people belong. But an additional reason for giving it so much attention is that it is a more controversial concept than it should be. Even though precise definitions of important concepts may not be a prerequisite of arriving at well-validated explanations in either natural or social science, sociology would undoubtedly be the better if we had a precise definition of power.

The starting-point – and this, at least, is not in dispute between sociologists of rival schools – is that as members of groups, communities, institutions and societies interacting with one another, people in some roles behave in some ways that they otherwise wouldn't because of the way other people in other roles behave towards them. But a choice immediately presents itself. Some sociologists prefer to use the concept of power only in circumstances where one person is compelled by another to do something against his or her will. On this view, power is explicitly contrasted with influence, enticement, persuasion, cajolery, guidance, encouragement or manipulation – that is, circumstances where the person who behaves differently from how he or she would otherwise behave does so either willingly or at any rate without being tempted by, or even perhaps aware of, an alternative. The difference is obviously a real one. If, as my feudal lord, you evict me from my cottage by force in order to hand it to another of your bondsmen, that's not at all the same thing as your approaching me as a property developer armed with planning permission and an open chequebook and making me an offer I can't refuse. But in both cases, it's because of your role that you're able to cause me to behave in a way that I otherwise wouldn't: it's imposed, rather than acquired or evoked, behaviour, even though I may be as happy to sell you my cottage because you've offered me so much money as to wear a hat like yours because I think you're a leader of fashion or to smile at you because I find you sexually attractive. It accordingly seems sensible to say that the difference between the two cases is that it's a different kind of power attaching to your role rather than that the first is an exercise of power and the second an exercise of something else.

But then how many kinds of power are there? Unfortunately, this question too is still controversial. In one sense, there are as many kinds of power as there are contexts within which the incumbents of different roles exercise it for their different purposes. But whatever the context, the exercise of power in the interaction between two or more people in their respective roles will involve the bringing to bear of either an inducement or a sanction. The relevant question, therefore, is not how many different kinds of conflict of interest provoke the exercise of power, but how many different kinds of inducements and sanctions there are when they do. The answer, as Weber recognized (although his discussion of it isn't as clear as it might be), is that there are three. Whatever the group, community, institution or society to which you and I both belong, if more power attaches to your role than mine there are three forms which the exercise of that power can take. Your power over me can be economic – that is, your role enables you either to endow me with, or deprive me of, wealth or income in money, services or goods; or it can be ideological – that is, your role enables you either to bestow on me, or take away from me, social esteem, honour or prestige; or it can be coercive – that is, your role enables you either to bring to bear on me, or protect me from, the exercise of physical force. From this, it follows that all societies have what can conveniently be called their modes of production, persuasion and coercion – that is, their distinctive ways of distributing and exercising economic, ideological and coercive power.

This may seem obvious. But there are many people (and some sociologists) who treat as distinctive kinds of power, and therefore dimensions of social structure, what are merely different attributes correlated with the possession of it. Education is the commonest example. People with educational qualifications, whatever these may be in their particular society, are likely on that account to be privileged over those without them. But in what does that privilege consist? To have read a lot of books, or passed an exam, or qualified for a diploma doesn't *in itself* give the person who has done these things power over those who haven't. It does so only if the institutional rules of the society are such that a person who has done them is on that account enabled to occupy and perform a role to which economic, ideological or coercive power attaches. Likewise, those sociologists who talk of ethnicity and gender as 'dimensions' of social inequality are guilty of a similar confusion. Men and women, or white-skinned people and black-skinned ones, have more or less power than each other not because a difference in power is inherent in either gender or ethnicity but because the institutional rules of their society make it so. The question which has still be to answered is: 'But what *kind* of power does the society give men because they are men or women because they are women, or white-skinned people because they are white-skinned or black-skinned people because they are black-skinned?' And the answer always comes back to one or more of the trio of economic, ideological and coercive power.

66

Matters, however, are made worse by a persistent habit among sociologists of contrasting power with wealth and/or prestige rather than recognizing that both wealth and prestige *are* power of a kind which is to be contrasted with coercive power. Here, for example, is an inextricably confused pair of sentences which I came across in a recent issue of the journal *Current Anthropology*:

> Social status as defined here reflects two usually related factors: power and wealth. Power is the ability to control resources, including other people and information, and is often a product of and a means to obtain wealth.[1]

The argument to which these sentences are a prelude is that in pre-Hispanic Oaxaca, in southern Mexico, the roles of the ideological elite, who held a monopoly of literary and astronomical knowledge, functioned to persuade the other members of the society to support them economically without being forcibly compelled to do so. It's an entirely convincing argument. Indeed, it's a textbook example of the need to relate economic, ideological and coercive power to one another in analysing the workings of a set of related institutions and the roles which constitute them. But what does it mean to say that power is the 'ability to control resources' and 'a means to obtain wealth' when wealth is itself ability to control resources? What about the control of people and information which comes from 'social status' in the sense of institutionalized esteem or prestige? How is 'control' of people exercised, and how is it to be equated with control of information? There could hardly be a clearer illustration of the lack of a precise definition of power, and of the benefits to be gained if only we had one.

On the other hand, there is a different and more substantial objection which is sometimes levelled against the threefold distinction between economic, ideological and coercive power. Granted, it can be said, that the three are connected but not reducible to one another, aren't there different forms of economic, ideological and coercive power which are similarly connected but irreducible? If the basic ingredients of human societies are the practices which define the roles by which their institutions are constituted, doesn't a further distinction have to be drawn between – to go no further – financial and commercial economic institutions, religious and secular ideological institutions, and military and administrative political institutions? And aren't these additional dimensions of structure and forms of power?

Well: it's perfectly true that within the same society there may be financial and commercial, religious and secular, or military and administrative roles which are in direct competition for power with one another, and any explanation of how the society functions or why it has evolved as it has will involve a recognition of it. But so far as the *forms* of power are concerned, the question remains the same one: are the inducements and sanctions attaching to any of these roles of some *other* kind than economic, ideological or coercive? And the answer is no. Financial roles may carry more or less power than commercial, religious than secular, or military than administrative: down the ages, bankers have sometimes reached the pinnacles of wealth only to be summarily expropriated, just as victorious generals have sometimes been summarily dismissed by civilian politicians. But the power that they carry doesn't rest on anything other than some combination of the three separate but related kinds of inducements and sanctions. If, as may well be the case, the anti-commercial financiers *also* have some coercive power, or the anti-clerical intellectuals *also* have some economic power, or the civilian officeholders *also* have some ideological power, that too may be critical to the explanation of the society's workings. But it happens because there can attach to the same role power of more than one kind, not because the role in which they are combined enables the person who occupies and performs it to deploy some new and different kind of inducement or sanction.

Nor is one kind of power any more fundamental or decisive

than the other two. Different sociologists, including not least Marx, Weber and Durkheim, have given different priority in their writings to each of them – Marx to the economic, Weber to the coercive, and Durkheim to the ideological. But it's not a question to be decided *a priori*. In some societies it's one and in others another. No sociologist studying the United States of America could fail to recognize the importance of the economic ('the business of America is business'). No sociologist studying the Indian system of caste could fail to recognize the importance of the ideological (inherited status, strict endogamy, rituals of purity and pollution). No sociologist studying the late Roman Republic could fail to recognize the importance of the coercive (political assassinations, slave revolts, mob violence, civil war). But to grasp the institutional workings of the particular society, let alone to explain why it has evolved as it has, you will always need to analyse the relation between the three.

'But to analyse the distribution of power oughtn't you to be able to measure it?' Yes, if you can. But sociologists can't measure the power of roles in the way that physicists can measure the power of heat engines. It's more a matter of formulating a clear set of concepts in terms of which comparisons can be drawn and devising a practical set of techniques with which to apply them – depending, as always, on what (exactly) you want to know, what kind of society you're looking at, and what evidence for the distribution and exercise of power within it is available to you.

The simplest, and probably the most familiar, representation of a society is as a triangle – a few powerful people at the top, rather more rather less powerful people in the middle, and the mass of the powerless at the bottom. By way of contrast, Aristotle's puta-tively stable society can then be represented as a broad, flattish diamond – a small elite, a big middle class, and a small category of powerless unfortunates at the bottom. A more sophisticated version, which I've taken from the American sociologist Gerhard E. Lenski's book *Power and Privilege*, is his representation of a 'typical agrarian society' which makes it look like Figure 1:[2]

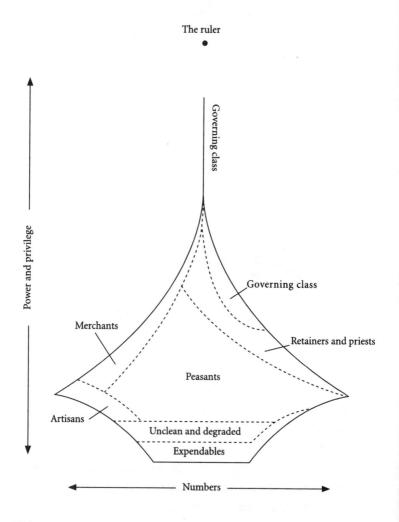

Figure 1

A lot more information is contained in a diagram like this than in a single triangle or diamond. But if, as I've insisted, there are three interrelated but mutually irreducible forms of power, then the constituent roles of any society whose distribution of economic, ideological and coercive power is to be measured will need to be represented three-dimensionally. This means that the logical way to visualize the social space within which more and less powerful roles are located is as the space enclosed between three co-ordinates joined at right angles; and since degrees of power are generally conceptualized in a metaphor which equates more power with a higher location and less power with a lower one, any society can be represented as an inverted pyramid and its constituent roles as vectors within it. A society (such as has never in fact existed) where there attached to a single role a monopoly of economic, ideological and political power and the rest of the population were all paupers, outcastes and slaves would then look like this:

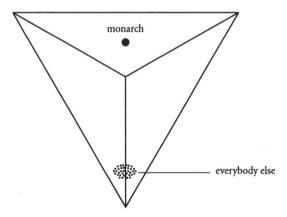

Figure 2

By contrast, a society (such as has never existed either) in which no roles to which there attached one kind of power had any power of the other two kinds would look like this:

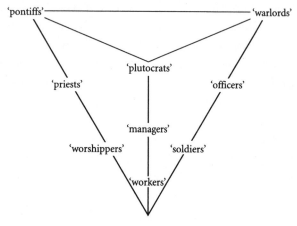

Figure 3

This, let me emphasize, is no more than a device to make vivid the three-dimensionality of social structure. Not only is it not possible to assign all the roles in any society precise places in a three-dimensional space and measure the distance between them in units of economic, ideological and coercive power, but diagrams like these can't reflect the fact that one person can occupy and perform more than one role, as well as move from one role to another. But I commend it to you, all the same, as a way of visualizing the differences between societies not only in degrees of inequality in the three dimensions but in the extent to which roles high or low in one dimension are higher or lower in another. In Lenski's agrarian society, do better-off peasants outrank lesser retainers and priests in prestige and political power as well as money? Are the unclean and degraded all poorer than any of the peasants and artisans? Don't even the lower echelons of the governing class have more prestige than the richer merchants? Only when questions like these have been asked and answered will it be possible to begin to offer a satisfactorily detailed analysis of the society's distinctive modes of production, persuasion and coercion.

Of more immediate practical value are a range of well-tried techniques for representing the distribution of power in the three dimensions separately. If you're studying a market society with a well-developed money economy, you're likely to want to plot the distribution of income shared among the society's members in accordance with their occupational roles; and when you do, you're likely to find that it looks much like this:

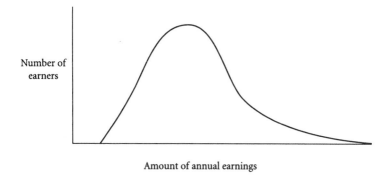

Amount of annual earnings

Figure 4

This is what any statistician will recognize as a familiar type of 'skewed' distribution with a long upper tail, as opposed to the 'normal', bell-shaped curve which fits the distribution of, for example, physical height. It's an even more interesting distribution than it may appear at first sight because it turns out to fit not only earnings but things like the size of firms and the ownership of private property across a surprisingly wide range of different societies. The British labour economist Henry Phelps Brown, in a lecture delivered in 1979, called it an 'unexplained uniformity'.[3] He didn't mean by this that it can't be accounted for as the mathematically predictable outcome of a cumulative sequence of differential probabilities, which is precisely what it is. He meant that he continued to find it surprising that it should fit the data as well as it has been known to do ever since the work of the Italian sociologist Vilfredo Pareto in the 1890s. Dispute it, denounce it, or deconstruct it as you will – and it does raise some complex issues about tax, retirement income, benefits in kind, and so forth – it is telling us a significant fact about how economic power is distributed in societies in which earnings are determined not by ideological or political institutions but by a labour market.

But suppose you're studying not an open market society but a village in Hindu India where ideological power is more important than economic and social status is apportioned in accordance with a ritual scale of permitted or prohibited contacts between the incumbents of hierarchically ordered roles. How can you possibly measure the inequality between them? Perhaps you can't. But perhaps you can construct a table of rows and columns which correlates the roles in order of rank with the forms of interaction permitted between them (such as handling the person's cooking utensils as opposed to touching the person's body). Or perhaps you can ask people to rank their roles against those of other people with whom they have dealings and then to say how they feel about different degrees of intimacy with them. It's true that, as with the young thieves pleading poverty in Chapter II, you'd better not be too ready to believe them. In an experiment carried out in the 1930s, the American sociologist R. T. Lapière showed that a hotel owner who said he would refuse admittance to a would-be guest whose ethnic status was defined by the dominant ideology as inferior might turn out to be surprisingly willing to do just that in a real-life situation where he had an empty room to fill and nobody else in sight to fill it.[4] But if the answers to your questions can be relied on, you might be able to draw up a diagram which would look something like this, and would thereby be illustrating something both intriguing and precise about the distribution of ideological power in the society in question:

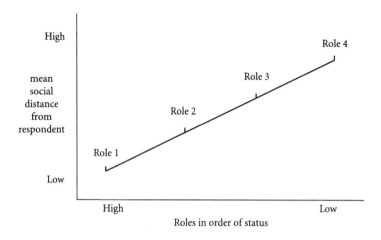

Figure 5

This still leaves coercive power, which is in some ways the most difficult to measure of all. But where the political or military institutions of a society are constituted by roles which are formally ranked in the way that governments and armies typically are, the organization chart will show you clearly who is empowered to give mandatory instructions to whom. It's true that such 'dominance hierarchies' are not always consistent: junior officers or officials may, for example, be empowered to inform on their immediate superiors to their superiors' superiors, in which case the organization chart neeeds to show a dotted line, representing a chain of communication in addition to the firm lines representing the chain of command. But it's still an objective depiction of the relative power of the roles concerned which rival sociologists disposed to question it can go out and check for themselves. The C-in-C can tell the General what to do, the General the Colonels, the Colonels the Captains, and the Captains the 'Poor Bloody Infantry' in the regiments over which the Captains hold their delegated commands:

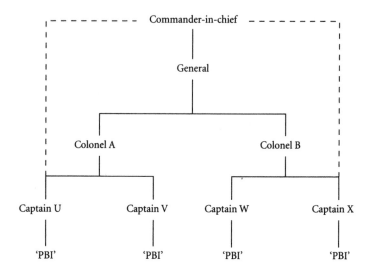

Figure 6

These are only three of the many techniques which sociologists have available to them for measuring, or at least representing, inequalities of power of the three kinds. More important for the purpose of this chapter is that when you've plotted a role-map of the group, community, institution or society which you're study-ing as best you can and measured the inequality of power between its constituent roles to whatever extent is technically feasible, you then face a further task which is fundamental to any analysis of how it works and why it has evolved into what it has. In the study of groups and face-to-face communities, the role-map can be plotted on an individual basis; even if the influence exerted by external institutions needs to be allowed for in explaining the pattern of social behaviour in the classroom, on the assembly line, at the office party, or on the board of the sociology department, the higher debates about the dynamics of class conflict, the circulation of elites, the reproduction of social inequality and so forth can be ignored. But you can't begin to explain the workings and evolution of institutions and societies as such without some sort of conceptual scheme in terms of which sets of roles similarly located in social space are distinguished from other such sets to which there attaches significantly more or less power, whether economic, ideological or coercive. You must, that is to say, draw some dividing-lines on your three-dimensional role-map, and have a theoretical criterion of some kind to justify drawing them where you do.

This is yet another important issue on which, unfortunately, sociologists of rival schools are as far apart as ever. Many, not all of whom would call themselves Marxists, are likely to say that societies are to be divided into a small number of more and less powerful 'classes'. Others are likely to say that 'class societies' are only one kind of society, to be contrasted with, for example, 'caste' societies or 'slave' societies where the power is allocated and the dividing-lines between roles therefore drawn on a quite different basis. Yet others are likely to say that societies should be analysed in terms of a continuum of power on which occupational roles, in particular, can be placed without any obvious dividing-line between one and the next. There is a broad consensus that in all societies roles (or, some would rather say, individuals or households or families) can be lumped together in categories which reflect a ranking of power (or, some would rather say, privilege or resources or life-chances) and that except, perhaps, in the case of the smallest and simplest it is therefore appropriate to see them as 'stratified'. But you will be lucky if you can find two different sociologists who agree about what exactly 'stratification' involves or how exactly its different aspects relate to one another, let alone what terms should be used for the clusters of roles or individuals or households or families which are located above or below each other in social space.

This doesn't matter too much as long as all these divergent approaches are directed to the common aim of reporting and explaining the distribution and exercise of power in the societies which the various authors have chosen to study. If there are three and only three separate dimensions of social stratification, then we need simply to preserve a distinction between them in whatever terminology is agreed to be least ambiguous and confusing. If we follow Weber's own usage, we shall talk about 'classes', 'status-groups' (the usual English translation of the German '*Stände*'), and 'parties'. The trouble with this, however, is that 'class' is used by most people, including many sociologists, in a much less precise sense, as likewise is 'status' (while the German term *Stand* is also the standard term for 'estate' in the sense of 'estate of the realm'); and 'party' normally denotes a political party like the Republican or Democratic parties in the United States or the Labour or Conservative parties in Britain, which is both more and less than what is wanted here. Besides, although the three forms of power are analytically distinct, they are always connected in practice. It must therefore be a good idea to try to find a word which is at the same time specific in denoting clusters of roles located above or below each other in social space and neutral between the dimension of social space in which they are so located. Since there isn't one, I found myself some years ago driven to invent one, and much as I dislike other people's neologisms I intend to use mine in the rest of this book. The word (whose derivation from the Greek implies a set of things or positions drawn up together in a rank) is 'systact'. I hope my use of it won't irritate you beyond endurance. But there just isn't any other concrete noun, least of all the irretrievably ambiguous 'class', which can do the job.

There is, to be sure, another way of approaching the whole issue, and that is to follow the terminology which people themselves use in talking about their society's modes of production, persuasion and coercion. Didn't I say myself in Chapter II that if there's a choice between 'their' terms and 'ours' we have to go for 'theirs'? People in all societies and cultures have words in their language for higher- and lower-ranked roles which reflect differences in wealth, prestige and influence, even if the inequalities between role and role are as nearly negligible as in the hunting and foraging bands. So perhaps that should be the starting-point. But to do so is to take the risk that (as I pointed out also in Chapter II) we may thereby be tied to a presumptive explanation of 'theirs' which is in fact mistaken. Stratification, admittedly, like any other aspect of our social relationships with the fellow-members of our common cultures and societies, is a matter not only of distances between roles in social space but of how we think about one another and accordingly behave to one another. But although, as always, we need to get sufficiently far inside 'their' heads to be sure that their actions have the meaning which we impute to them, one of the most reliable findings which comes out of research into what sociologists sometimes call 'subjective stratification' is that people are woefully ignorant about how power actually *is* exercised and distributed among the roles of which their societies consist. What's more, it's often the people at the top, who might be thought to know better, who have even less realistic views than the people at the bottom who suffer directly from the exercise of the power attaching to the roles of the people at the top: the Persian King Ardeshir, who lumped all 'cultivators, menials etc.' into a single omnibus systact out of the four into which he divided his society, carefully ranked 'religious leaders and guardians of the fire-temples' in the second and 'physicians, scribes, and astrologers' in the third.[5] So we have not only to be careful how we use the vernacular categories of the people whose patterns of social behaviour we are observing, but also to be ready to jettison their explanations of it as soon as our observations of their behaviour so require. 'We' and 'they' can agree if nothing else that it's all about the power which attaches to different roles. But what power, where acquired, how exercised, and why distributed as it is are questions for objective sociological analysis, not folk wisdom.

What, then, can we say that we know about the distribution and exercise of power in human societies in general? What distinctive contribution can sociologists make?

One plausible-looking answer might appear to be that there is more and more power about as social evolution goes on and on. Although we know that no society is completely egalitarian, we also know that the most egalitarian are in general the least complex. But inequality of power is a relative matter. In a simple society where everyone is miserably poor but one household has some rudimentary furniture and utensils, the standard statistical measure of inequality will yield a score higher than for the contemporary United States. In a simple society where everyone treats everyone else as equals except that one ritual specialist is credited with supernatural gifts of divination, that person may enjoy as much relative prestige as Louis XIV ever did at Versailles. In a simple society where there is no ruling group with a monopoly of force, a deviant accused of sorcery may be as defenceless against the threat of assassination as a deviant in the Soviet Union accused of counter-revolutionary tendencies against the threat of summary execution at the hands of the KGB. To cite a gruesome recent example, a well-documented account of the genocidal policy of the Pol Pot regime in Cambodia by the American historian Ben Kiernan concludes that despite (or should it be because of?) Cambodia's relatively underdeveloped economy, that regime 'probably exerted more power over its citizens than any state in world history'.[6]

If, therefore, there is a well-validated sociological generalization to be formulated about the relation between the distribution of power in human societies and the total of economic, ideological and coercive resources available for distribution, it isn't one which states that 'equality' is inversely proportionate to 'progress'. It is simply false to assert that the less resources there are, the more equally they will always be shared. But there may be other pertinent, non-vacuous generalizations which can be more convincingly advanced. So let's see what we can do. The most relevant to this chapter is to the effect that 'descent with modification' requires some things to happen before others – a proposition which, so stated, looks like the platitude of the century, but isn't. Its point is that although social evolution isn't a series of progressive stages through which all institutions and societies have to pass in a prede-termined sequence, it is nevertheless a process in which *some* moves from one kind of society, and therefore one set of modes of pro-duction, persuasion and coercion to another, are ruled out. In natural selection, it would be very odd to find in the fossil record a sequence in which elephants came before bacteria. In cultural selection, it would be very odd to find in the archaeological record a sequence in which Beethoven's symphonies came before the bone flutes found in late Stone Age burial sites. In social selection, it would be very odd to find in the ethnographic record a sequence in which bureaucratic nation-states came before communities gov-erned by village elders or kin-group chiefs. 'Descent with modifi-cation' proceeds by a sort of branching along alternative evolutionary pathways of which some are dead-ends, some are turning-points, some run in parallel, some turn back on them-selves, some rejoin others, and some lead to wider and some to narrower choices of onward route. But the increasing range and complexity of the alternatives both widens and narrows the range of ways of exercising and distributing power which remain on offer, and sociologists of all persuasions can agree that some theoretical possibilities can be categorically ruled out. This is nowhere clearer than on the topic with which philosophers writing about power were exercised long before sociologists started doing the same: the origins of the state.

Once again, there is a terminological problem. Definitions of 'the state' have been and still are disputed up hill and down dale by philosophers and sociologists alike. But we can all recognize one as soon as we come upon a society with roles to which there attaches a continuing centralized monopoly of the means of coercion independently of household or family relationships. So how do they come into being on their own – when, that is, there aren't any others around to be imitated, allied with, or surrendered to? Sociologists call this 'primary' as opposed to 'secondary' state formation, and although it has happened at more than one place and time in the course of social evolution, there aren't that many cases of it – perhaps only Egypt, North India, Mesopotamia, China, West Africa, Mexico and Peru. The sequence of events (so far as we can reconstruct them) is different in each. But somehow or other there emerge within hitherto 'stateless' societies the permanent specialized roles to which there attaches enforceable power to direct or constrain the activities of the society's other members. For that to happen, there does have to be an aggregation of the resources from which that power derives. The soldiers and officials have to be well enough armed to compel obedience, well enough rewarded to carry out their functions, and well enough motivated for their loyalty to be sustained. And once the mutation of practices has come about and the evolutionary trick been turned, there open up the possibilities for rapid and cumulative accretions of power which can lead either to the formation of enormous empires or, on the contrary, to long-lasting semi-stable equilibria among groups of little states none of which succeeds in dominating the others.

Societies in which power is stably distributed don't have to be states. Those which have evolved into statehood may aggregate and deploy greater concentrations of power than societies which haven't. But those which haven't can be just as stable, if not more so. How so? Not because they're in a condition of anarchic bliss in which any form of discipline – or, as sociologists are apt to call it, 'social control' – is redundant. It's because there are other ways of keeping people in order outside the immediate family and household than through the apparatus of statehood.

If you look at the role-maps of the numerous societies in the ethnographic and historical record of which this is true, you will find a range of practices and roles in which the incumbents of subordinate roles accept without serious resistance the authority of their designated superiors. It may be surprising, at first sight, that this obedience can be successfully imposed without soldiers, policemen, magistrates, viziers, shoguns, governors, inquisitors or satraps to whom the means of coercion are delegated by the incumbents of roles constitutive of a central state which holds a monopoly of them. But the answer is to be found in a distinction about which Marshall Sahlins has written to particularly good effect. It is the distinction, as Sahlins puts it, between *coming to* power – i.e., entering a role to which power is institutionally attached – and *constructing* power – i.e., using a role as a means to increasing the power attaching to it. This isn't a hard-and-fast distinction. But it marks a very big difference. Contrast the President of the United States with the *reth*, as he is called, of the Shilluk of the Upper Nile. Whoever gets elected President of the United States, however unimpressive as a person, is then in a position of great, albeit far from unlimited, power. The uncharitable columnist who described Richard M. Nixon as a little guy in a crumpled suit who jumps out of the closet and runs around shouting 'I wannabe President' was making this very point: the power is there to be come to, however unprepossessing the aspirant. But the *reth* of the Shilluk, although he is a hereditary 'king', has powers only of mediation, not of compulsion: no matter how impressive a person he is (and he needs to be), the incumbents of the other constituent roles of Shilluk society are free to ignore his wishes if they so please.[7]

There is, accordingly, a continuum of power, as Sahlins demonstrates by contrasting the societies of Melanesia and Polynesia, neither of which evolved into statehood. The Melanesian 'big man' is more than the leader of a small, egalitarian, food-sharing band of hunters or foragers: he commands a following extending well beyond his immediate family and household, he has several wives and large gardens, he dispenses pigs, vegetables and shells in quantity to his followers and dependants, he is an eloquent orator, a courageous fighter, and a shrewd diplomatist. But unlike a Polynesian 'paramount chief', he is not the head of a large conical clan, he controls no body of soldiers, attendants, administrators or supervisors, he is not credited with *mana* by virtue of divine descent, and he is economically more dependent on his followers than they on him. A Melanesian 'big man' who tries to behave as if he was a Polynesian 'paramount' will be ignored, ridiculed, deserted, or even (occasionally) killed. Yet the Hawaiian 'paramount' is still not a 'head of state' like the President of the United States. No doubt he would like to be. But he can't apply the means of coercion over a sufficient distance, he can't transcend the boundaries of kinship, he can't raise taxes or tribute sufficient to support a permanent administrative staff, and he can't eliminate the endemic risk of rebellion.[8] So it's not as platitudinous as it may seem to say that (i) there are some critical transitions in the distribution and exercise of power which (ii) not all societies will necessarily make, but (iii) will have some irreversible consequences for the society when they do and (iv) can only be explained with hindsight by seeing what mutations in the practices defining the society's constituent roles made the transition possible and what features of the environment in which they did so then made it last.

You may think that this is still not saying much. But twentieth-century sociologists and anthropologists can justifiably claim to have resolved a central argument about the distribution and exercise of power in human societies which goes back some three hundred years in European political thought: the argument between Hobbes and Rousseau about the so-called 'state of nature'. Neither of the two was doing (or wanted to do) the kind of sociology this book is about. They were, on the contrary, attitude-peddling for all they were worth. But since they were both AMs of genius, they effectively set the agenda for sociologists as well as philosophers concerned with the question whether human societies are, or originally were, peaceable until violent or violent until peaceable. Hobbes is as famous for positing a natural state of society in which there is a war of all against all until power is vested in a sovereign authority which enforces peace as Rousseau is famous for positing a natural state of society in which noble savages live in harmony and contentment until corrupted by a fatal urge for domination over one another. Both Hobbes and Rousseau were, as Nietzsche was to do, composing just-so stories to justify their moral and political preferences. But the two alternative stories pose a question which sociology, if it has anything interesting to say about power, has to be capable of answering in its own terms. Which is right? Are we peaceable until violent? Or violent until peaceable?

The correct answer, which was already implicit in some of what I said in Chapter I, is: neither. From the earliest stages of human, or for that matter hominid, evolution, our ancestors were simultaneously involved in *both* co-operative *and* antagonistic relations with one another. For all our lack of direct evidence for the patterns of social behaviour of 50,000 years ago, we can say with confidence that neither a Hobbesian nor a Rousseauesque state of nature ever existed in fact. But we can say more than that. And it needs to be said, not least because there are still some sociologists and anthropologists around who are either neo-Hobbesian or neo-

Rousseauesque AMs – who, that is, maintain either that warfare is and always has been a human universal and that anyone who denies it is a utopian sentimentalist, or that only because societies which had evolved into statehood imposed their wicked practices on the pristine societies of America, Africa and Asia did the intruders observe behaviour for which their own violent incursions were responsible.

The truth of the matter is that, whatever Hobbes may have thought, there are a few simple societies which don't engage in warfare at all and where violence is consistently avoided and condemned; and, whatever Rousseau may have thought, the practice of lethal violence within and between simple societies where the intrusion of alien imperialists is out of the question can be abundantly documented – including archaeological evidence of the killings of children as well as adults by stone axes or arrowheads from prehistoric sites in Europe, America (including the Canadian Arctic), and, in a particularly striking case dated about 12,000 BC, Upper Egypt.[9] But then what about those genuinely peaceable societies, however few they may be, whose members prefer flight to fight? And what about the truces, treaties, alliances and armistices which limit the Hobbesian war of all against all even between societies which are unmistakably warlike? And what about once warlike societies which have managed to evolve into models of neutrality?

These questions can only be answered by looking at the role-map of the societies in question and seeing how the practices defining their constituent roles relate to their environment. When you do, and when you've analysed their distribution and exercise of power in detail, you will find that the question whether human societies are 'fundamentally' peaceable or violent is even more misconceived than ever. Take a people called the Semai, of whom there are about 15,000 scattered along the river valleys of central Malaysia. The Semai are reported by two different American anthropologists who have lived among them, Robert Dentan and Clayton Robarchek, as exceptionally non-violent. Not only do they not engage in warfare, but they eschew violence in their interpersonal relations, they bring up their children not to be aggressive, they deplore the norms and values of their more aggressive neighbours, and they concede to their headmen powers of mediation only, not of coercion, in internal disputes. But when young Semai males were recruited by the British in the 1950s to fight against Communist guerrillas, they were as bloodthirsty as anybody else. Yes, but they were then removed from their normal environment; when they came back, they were as peaceable as before. But how can we be sure that they are quite such strangers to violence in any form as they tell visiting American anthropologists they are (remember Margaret Mead and the teenage Samoan girls)? So let's test the hypothesis that, despite their protestations, their murder rate is not significantly lower than a lot of other people's. Guess what – it looks like it isn't. The exact numbers are hard to establish, but the Semai are not an exception to the rule that there is no known human society in which one person has never deliberately killed another. And if they run away instead of fighting when their aggressive neighbours attack them, isn't that simply because of their unhappy experience of successive defeats at their neighbours' hands and the availability of unused but cultivable land which they can run away to? Game, set and match to Hobbes.

Or is it? Although I've simplified the argument to the point of caricature, the interesting general point has been made by another American anthropologist, Bruce Knauft, whose own fieldwork has been done among the unwarlike but highly murderous Gebusi of New Guinea (683 murders per year per 100,000 people). An avoidance of warfare, a stated disapproval of violence, and even a low overall incidence of interpersonal aggression are, it would appear, quite compatible with a high ratio of lethal violence to aggression. And if you want an explanation of how *that* can come about, the answer in the Gebusi case lies in the combination of a belief in sorcery as a cause of death (and therefore frequent accusations to that effect) with the animosity which inevitably arises in a sister-exchange marriage system in which young males are seeking to acquire the mate of their choice without actually having to give a chosen sister in exchange – a textbook example of how the function of a society's constituent roles is explained by the competitive selection of the practices defining them.[10]

This last example, no less than any other which I might have chosen to illustrate the inextricable combination of co-operation and aggression in all human societies, also illustrates the paradox which runs through this whole discussion about the exercise of power by the incumbents of interacting roles. It's because individu-ally different people are, on the whole, consistent performers of their roles in their different cultures and societies that their social behaviour is as explicable as it is by the sociologists and anthropolo-gists who study them. Warlords behave like warlords, soldiers behave like soldiers, big-men behave like big-men, paramounts behave like paramounts, presidents behave like presidents. But to point this out is to restate a paradox in the same breath as the platitude – the paradox being that our social behaviour is as reliably patterned as our individual behaviour is unmanageably diverse. Not only is the future course of social evolution unpredictable, but the particular decisions and consequent actions of different people in their roles are only possible to forecast either in very broad terms or under very restricted conditions. True as it may be to say that sociology is all about the rules which govern the distribution and exercise of power in societies of different kinds, explanation at the level of social integration, just as much as at the level of system integration, is possible only with the benefit of hindsight. As the American sociologist James S. Coleman points out in his *Foundations of Social Theory*, sociologists seem to regard people as on the one hand obedient conformists performing their roles in the ways that the authorities to which they are subordinated expect, yet on the other as the spontaneous, disorderly and unpredictable creatures which (when not doing sociology) we all think of ourselves as being.[11] So how do we reconcile the two? Are we in control of our own actions or aren't we?

These questions lead straight into what sociologists call the 'micro-macro' problem. This can be approached in a number of different ways, including both controlled experiments from the psychology lab and game-theoretical models from the blackboard. But just as there is no incompatibility at the general level between evolutionary psychology and theories of rational choice, so do the different approaches to the 'micro-macro' problem all reinforce the conclusion that, through whatever internal psychological process, human beings as social animals are inveterate conformists. The differences between people don't undermine the consistencies between roles. However weird and wacky we may be in the conduct of our private lives, once we are out there acting socially as members of groups, communities, institutions and societies we are much more likely than not to adhere to the good old maxim of doing, when in Rome, what the Romans do.

Of the evidence of conformism which comes from the psychology lab, the two most famous (and to many people, disturbing) findings are those of the Asch and Milgram experiments.[12] In the Asch experiment, the experimental subjects are induced to mistrust the evidence of their senses by the unanimous testimony of others who (unbeknownst to them) have been primed by the experimenters to give deliberately false answers about the relative lengths of straight lines drawn on cards. In the Milgram experiment, the subjects are induced to administer what they mistakenly believe to be painful electric shocks to fellow-subjects in what they have been told by a person in authority is a study of how punishment affects learning. As with all such experiments, those dismayed by their results can (and do) argue that the experimental subjects are not a representative sample of human beings as such and that people in other societies and cultures wouldn't behave in the same way. But the onus is on the critics. If Margaret Mead doesn't want to believe it, she'd better get back to Samoa and bring home a conflicting set of equally incontrovertible experimental findings. What's more, in follow-ups to the Milgram experiment, it has been shown that people are consistently disposed to discount or misinterpret it. We don't, it would seem, want to face up to just how conformist we are: we systematically underestimate the strength of the external pressures to which we yield in our apparently spontaneous decisions about how to behave in company. The choice may be in the individual mind, but the power is in the social group.

Of the evidence which comes from the game theorists' blackboards (or rather computers), some of the most striking is directed to modelling the behaviour of people in crowds. Game theory is a branch of mathematics which was expected by its principal founder, the brilliant John von Neumann, to be of particular value to economists. But it can also be applied to behaviour of the kind which many readers of this chapter may have observed and perhaps even experienced: individual behaviour which gets drowned, as it were, in a tide of collective action. Coleman's own discussion draws the important distinction between panics, in which the objective is to escape something nasty, and riots, in which the objective is to do something nasty to somebody else; and there is also the related distinction to be drawn between crowds in which you need to act independently of others (e.g. a depositors' run on a bank) and in which you need to act with them (e.g. a lynch mob). But Coleman shows clearly that occasions where orderly behaviour within a context of apparently stable authority relationships gives way to apparent irrationality can be much better explained by mathematical analysis of alternative rewards to the individual member of the crowd than by appeal to an irrational 'mob psychology'. Once again, there is no inconsistency between the evolutionary approach and rational choice theory: formal models of the behaviour of crowds in the different environments in which it is or is not rewarding for the individual to transfer the power of decision to others do convincingly fit the observed behaviour of different kinds of crowd. Needless to say, you don't have to look far in the academic literature before you find articles with titles like 'On the Inadequacy of Game Theory for the Solution of Real-World Collective Action Problems'.[13] But neither Coleman nor any of the other sociologists and psychologists who have done important work in this area has ever claimed that it explains everything about collective behaviour. The remarkable thing is that it explains as much as it does.

Perhaps the resistance to game-theoretic analyses of collective behaviour, as to experiments of the Asch and Milgram kind, is just another symptom of the general reluctance of people to accept that actions which are so (as they feel) impregnably and even defiantly autonomous should be so amenable to scientific explanation in terms of the power which some people have over others. Look at all the different goals we choose for ourselves, the different standards of behaviour which we set ourselves, and the diverse stratagems we contrive in order to advance our conflicting interests! Agreed: indeed we do. But studied in the aggregate, our behaviour falls into patterns formed not by the goals and schemes themselves but by the interpersonal and institutional environment within which we are motivated to conceive them. The sociologists who call themselves 'ethnomethodologists' and who, in reaction to the platitudes of grand theory, set themselves to document in detail the way we monitor and adjust our face-to-face interactions with each other, have convincingly shown just how competent as well as active we all are in managing these interactions to our own advantage.[14] But it is this common pursuit of individual advantage by whatever diverse means which explains, when analysed in depth, why the pattern of relations of power between role and role which emerges out of them is not idiosyncratic at all. It's true that not every incumbent of every role conforms to the pattern. In all societies and cultures there are misfits, cranks, rebels, saints, heroes, dropouts and mavericks. But in all societies and cultures, they are the exception, not the rule. Most people at most times in most places and on most occasions behave towards one another in ways which, whether the behaviour is evoked, acquired or imposed, is a consistent reflection of the relative power of their respective roles and the practices by which those roles are defined.

V

Matters of Chance

ON 10 OCTOBER 1940 an editorial in *The Times* pronounced that 'no more unlikely pattern of events could have been predicted' than that which brought Winston Churchill to the leadership of the British Conservative Party. But what exactly was the newspaper seeking to convey to its readers in saying so? Not that the pattern of events was inexplicable. On the contrary: many pages of historical and biographical writing have been devoted since then to explaining it. But the more detailed the narrative, the clearer it is that *The Times* was right. Who could possibly have foreseen in 1935, when the last British pre-war general election was held, that this hard-drinking sixty-year-old maverick politician, marginalized as he then was within a party which he had rejoined eleven years earlier after deserting it twenty years before that, would be the next-but-one successor to a leader with whom he was even more at odds over foreign than over domestic policy?

Yet the wild improbability of Churchill's career is no wilder than that of many others, from Julius Caesar to Bill Clinton – to say nothing of Chingiz Khan, emerging from obscurity among the disputatious tribes of twelfth-century Mongolia to become, by the time of his death in 1227, the most successful conqueror ever known in the history of the world. Is it surprising that Chingiz should have believed, as he apparently did, that his success was divinely inspired? But what feels like predestination to the person in question is apt to look to the detached observer uncommonly like luck.

Yes, but what is luck? If you play a card game like bridge, in which all 52 cards in the pack are in play, you will probably have wondered what it would be like to pick up a hand consisting of nothing but spades, while at the same time correctly assuming that it isn't actually going to happen to you. But you will also know that the odds against it are no different from the odds against your picking up whatever hand you've actually been dealt. From the moment that you sit down at the card table, you are launched into a series of wildly improbable events: the number of possible distributions of 52 cards between four players is a mind-boggling 8.065×10^{67}. Given that the rules of bridge are what they are, you can fairly be said to be lucky if you are dealt a series of 'strong' hands and unlucky if you are dealt a series of 'weak' ones. But from another standpoint, it's misleading twice over to put it that way. In the first place, you will be dealt just as many strong hands as weak ones if you go on playing long enough; and in the second, each deal, however unpredictable, is the determinate outcome of how the pack was shuffled and cut. So it can be said that the hand you pick up both is and isn't 'random', depending how you want to apply that term.

I am not, of course, implying that human history has been one long card game. The analogy isn't between social life and a rubber of bridge but between the part played by chance in both of them. As societies and institutions continue to evolve, and as the incumbents of economic, ideological and political roles go on competing with one another for power, things are and will always be happening which are just as unpredictable as the distribution of the cards in a bridge game. But *something* has to happen; *somebody* had to be the British Prime Minister in 1940; and once something has, and somebody is, things will turn out somehow in a different way from that in which they otherwise would. So when sociologists, as opposed to historians, look at what I shall call GBEs (Great Big Events) like the First and Second World Wars, or the French or

Russian revolutions, they are less interested in plotting the sequence of wildly improbable events which furnishes the explanation of their occurrence than in identifying the structural and cultural conditions which, given that one rather than another sequence of wildly improbable events *had* occurred, explains why their consequences for the modes of production, persuasion and coercion of the societies involved were what they were.

Take the French Revolution. There is, and will no doubt continue to be, intense debate among historians about the relative significance of the many events and circumstances which can plausibly be argued to have contributed to its occurrence, course and outcome. What if the government's finances had been in better shape, or the harvests less disastrous, or the Bastille hadn't fallen, or the King had been stronger-willed, or the Réveillon riots had never happened because the *gardes françaises* hadn't let the Duchesse d'Orléans' coach, which shouldn't have been there in the first place, through the barricades? Elementary probability theory tells us that where a set of unrelated events have a specified chance of occurring, the likelihood that all of them will occur is to be calculated by multiplying the chances of their occurring separately: the chance of throwing a six with one die is 1 in 6, but the chance of throwing a double 6 with two dice is 1 in 36. So imagine what a figure we would arrive at if we could assign separate probabilities to all the individual events whose unpredictable combination brought about the overthrow of the *ancien régime*! But the French Revolution is what actually happened, just like the cards you were actually dealt when you sat down at the bridge table. And some historians, as well as sociologists, would be willing to agree that once given the state of the government's finances and of France's economic and political institutions in general, *something* was bound to occur which sooner or later would have caused France to evolve into the sort of society which it in fact became when the Revolution was over.[1] So if you want to know whether the French Revolution was a 'matter of chance' or not, the answer has to be both yes and no. Yes, because of its unlikelihood. No, because of the likelihood that some other conjunction of improbable events would have occurred which would, given the condition of France, have had similar long-term effects in making its constituent groups, communities and institutions the kinds of groups, communities and institutions that they became.

Either way, nobody will dispute that GBEs divert the course of social evolution from the pathway it would otherwise have followed. But so can what I shall call tlms (tiny little mutations). Although tlms are happening all the time, most of them don't lead anywhere. But some have consequences out of all proportion to their size. They are perhaps most obvious in the field of technology, where the dedicated pursuit of innovation at every level of detail generates a proliferation of novel designs for anything from cooking utensils to spacecraft, and where their acceptance or rejection through a sequential process of trial and error is immediately reminiscent of natural selection itself. But they don't need to be the products of conscious design. Or even if they are, their long-term effects may be quite different from what the original innovator expected or wished. So although it's evidently false to say that they arise 'by chance', it's true to say that they might as well have, since their success depends not on how passionately the innovator hoped, or even confidently predicted, that they would catch on but on how far the environment in which they emerged favoured their doing so.

In cultural evolution, the mutations can be very tiny indeed. Somebody takes an unreflecting decision one day to wear a baseball cap back to front, and the next thing you know every kid on the block is doing it. One day in 1810, Beau Brummell goes out with his cravat carelessly tied, and next morning every fashionable young man in London is deliberately careless in tying his cravat. But social evolution is sometimes not very different. Somebody says to somebody one day, 'suppose you come and work for me and I reward you in cash at the end of the period' and the other person agrees. The next thing you know the practice of wage-labour is transforming the mode of production. Or maybe it isn't. In ancient Greek tradition, wage-labour goes all the way back to the time when the gods Poseidon and Apollo worked for a year for Laomedon, King of Troy, for a wage agreed in advance which Laomedon then refused to pay – *not* a clever thing to do at the best of times, and certainly not when you've hired a couple of gods (as Laomedon soon found out). But as it happened, wage-labour never came to dominate the Greek economy. It coexisted with slavery and other forms of unfree labour, both male and female, whose functions explain a lot more about the evolution of the societies of Ancient Greece than wage-labour does. If you want a *genetic* explanation of the origin of Greek slavery, you will find that somebody on the Aegean island of Chios in the eighth century B C was probably the first to think of selling captives as slaves rather than either killing or ransoming them, and it would be intriguing to find out who as well as where. But no sociological analysis of the evolution and function of slavery in the Ancient Greek world depends on knowing the answer. Likewise, it makes no difference to the sociology of early medieval Europe who were the first lord and the first vassal to enter into a formal relationship of commendation and protection, or to the sociology of the late medieval Italian city-states who was the first elective consul, or to the sociology of tenth-century Japan who was the first samurai to attach himself to a regional lord at the expense of the power of the central government. It just happened to be who it happened to be, with what then turned out to be some pretty momentous consequences.

A good illustration which, like my handshaking example in Chapter II, isn't as trivial as it looks, is the kilt – that curious garment which has probably given rise to more bad jokes than any other item of human apparel in recorded history. To a sociologist, its interest is in its function in helping to divert the military potential of young male Highlanders from the service of a Jacobite Pretender to the service of British imperial expansion – to which, as it turned out, the kilted Highland regiments made a notable contribution. To an anthropologist, its interest is in its function as a symbol of romantic nationalism among the Scottish gentry and its rise into civilian as well as military fashion at the time of King George IV's state visit to Edinburgh. To a sociobiologist, its interest is as a striking and unusual item of apparel which, as with the apparel of the warriors and hunters of earlier societies and cultures, could function to enhance the warrior's reproductive fitness by making him an object of attention to potentially childbearing women. But it's equally irrelevant to them all that, contrary to subsequent claims by pious Scottish nationalists that the kilt was traditionally worn in the communities from which the Highland regiments were recruited, it was in fact devised in the late 1720s by an English Quaker industrialist named Thomas Rawlinson as a cheap and convenient garment for his workmen.[2] It's as haphazard a tlm, therefore, as any in natural selection – explicable, as genetic mutations are, in its own terms at a different level, but so far as its evolutionary consequences are concerned, just as much a 'matter of chance'.

But chance enters into sociological analysis in other ways besides the occurrence of the events which turn out, however improbably, to influence the subsequent course of social evolution. No less than in the physical and biological sciences, statistical theory can be used to generate testable explanations not of specific events but of their probability. The insurance company with which you've taken out your life policy doesn't know in what year you're going to die, and its consulting actuaries aren't going to waste time trying to predict it. But they can tell you with a high degree of precision what the *chances* are of your living to a given age. And their ability to do so is being tested year after year: if they were wrong, their company's Life and Pensions Department would have lost so much money by now that it would have been either taken over or closed down.

Yes, I know. There are lies, damned lies and statistics. But a statistic, like a gun, is as good or bad as the person who uses it. Properly applied, statistical theory is an extraordinarily powerful instrument in the hands of natural and social scientists alike. I say 'extraordinarily' because much of what it teaches us is at odds (no pun intended) with what passes for common sense. Although we are by now used to opinion polls which confidently report the state of mind of the whole of the voting, or viewing, or purchasing public on the basis of interviews with a tiny-looking sample of them, it's still remarkable just how much information can confidently be extrapolated from how little data. Most people have little or no grasp of probability theory, little capacity for the rational estimation of risk, and an obstinate reluctance to accept even such irrefutable propositions as that, as Adam Smith pointed out two centuries ago, you're not increasing but reducing your chance of making money if you buy two lottery tickets instead of one: you've doubled the sum you're virtually certain to lose in return for a minuscule increase in the negligible chance that you'll be the winner. Historians of sociology are sometimes a little patronizing about the statistical naivety of the British pioneers, in particular, of quantitative social research. Charles Booth, in the monumental study of poverty in London which he brought out in seventeen volumes between 1889 and 1903, didn't use sampling at all, and Seebohm Rowntree, whose study of poverty in York, published in 1901, was even more influential, didn't use it as efficiently as he might. I myself have to admit that I continue to find the Law of Large Numbers counterintuitive, and continue to be amazed at how small a random sample will yield how reliable a set of conclusions about the distribution of whatever characteristic it may be in the total population sampled. And I continue, too, to be awed by the precision with which statisticians are able to calculate the unlikelihood that a given correlation between variables is spurious, or the chances that a specified proportion of a specified population will be a specified distance above or below the average on a quantified variable. Of course statistical techniques can be ignorantly or carelessly or dishonestly applied. But without them, we should be even more at a loss to account for complex patterns of human social behaviour than we are; and it is (to me, at least) a matter of astonishment that there are universities which award degrees in sociology to students who've not been required to pass an exam even in elementary statistical methods.

Perhaps the resistance of so many people to the application of statistical methods to human social behaviour is just another symptom of the more general reluctance to accept that our spontaneous decisions and idiosyncratic actions are amenable to scientific explanation at all. 'I'm not a statistic, I'm a human being!' Faced with the overwhelming evidence that smoking causes lung cancer, don't we immediately think of Uncle Jim who inhaled two packs a day for decades on end and died of unrelated causes at the age of 90? But a reaction like this has no more to do with the validity of either the methods or the findings in question than did Bishop Wilberforce's horror at the proposition that he was descended from an ape – and, as we now know, an African ape at that. More to the point is that, as every textbook on statistical methods rightly proclaims, 'correlation is no proof of causation'. This, you may say, is just another platitude. Few if any readers of this paragraph will need to have explained to them the point of jokes like 'since age is correlated with political attitudes, voters' ages are obviously caused by the way they vote', or 'since people get hangovers after drinking either brandy and soda or whisky and soda, soda water obviously causes hangovers'. Nor do you need much sophistication in these matters to be rightly suspicious of sociologists who run their data through the computer every way they can think of in order then to claim that their statistically significant correlations amount to causal explanations which have been successfully tested against attempted invalidation in accordance with the best scientific method. But there is, all the same, an important lesson to be learned here. As I've insisted already, serious sociology has to furnish the *reason* for which a presumptively causal correlation *is* causal; and no statistical technique, however refined, will do that for you. The famous French philosopher Jean-Paul Sartre is on record as pronouncing that 'statistics can never be dialectics'. To me, that's not merely an unnecessary but a foolish thing to say, even though to another French philosopher, Jaques Ellul, it is 'profound'.[3] But as with Roy Porter's remark, which I quoted at the end of Chapter I, that the success of evolutionary theory is a 'political project', I think I can see what Sartre was getting at. If, as Sartre believed, the right kind of theory with which to explain the course of human history is a 'dialectical' theory of a Marxist kind, it isn't by way of statistical calculations that you're going to arrive at it. As it happens, 'dialectics' *isn't* the right kind of theory with which to explain the course of human history, whereas statistics, if properly used, are of far more genuine explanatory value to sociology than anything in Sartre's *Critique de la raison dialectique*. But, yes: the theory does have to be imported from somewhere else.

The trouble, however, is the enormous scope which both the application and the analysis of sociological statistics provide for the Attitude-Merchants. In societies like ours, statistics about anything from the chance of being killed in a road accident to trends in net bank lending to figures for movie-going, house-moving, beer-drinking, and live births outside marriage are churned out in indigestible quantities every year by government, academic and freelance researchers alike. Many of them bear directly on controversial issues of public policy, and many are in fact deployed in support of policies which are actually put into effect. But, for that very reason, the temptation – to 'policy-oriented' academics no less than to party politicians – to play fast and loose is often too much for human frailty to withstand.

Take crime statistics. They have just about everything wrong with them. The definitions of the various offences which the law subsumes under the rubric of 'crime' are notoriously ambiguous. Much crime goes undetected, and much goes unreported because neither its victims nor (obviously) its perpetrators report it to the authorities. If it's reported locally, the figures eventually published will be a lot lower than if it's reported centrally: you don't need a degree in criminology to know that a precinct captain in Chicago has an interest in presenting to his superiors a crime rate which is as flattering to him as he can massage it into being. If and when defendants charged with a serious offence under the British or American system of criminal justice are arrested and tried, an unascertainable proportion of them will be acquitted by juries even though they did in fact commit the offence and another unascertainable proportion will be convicted even though they didn't. Different categories of potential or presumptive offenders may be very differently treated by law enforcement agencies, notably the members of ethnic minorities: how will it ever be possible to tell how far their statistical over-representation in the courts and cells of Britain and the United States reflects criminality on their part and how far it reflects discrimination on the part of judges, juries and police? And even if the figures are trustworthy, how on earth can they be interpreted correctly? When political argument is raging, as it has for centuries, over whether it is true or false to say that 'prison works', what are we to make of a study by the British Home Office's Research Unit which calculates that a 25% increase in imprisonment is required to reduce the number of offences by 1%? I take the example from a parliamentary exchange in 1997 between the Lord Chief Justice of England and

Wales and the government minister responsible for replying to him. Was the minister persuaded by the LCJ? Of course not. She replied: 'That research was based on an across the board, untargeted increase in the prison population. By contrast, our proposals are carefully targeted at persistent offenders and can therefore be expected to have a much more significant effect on prison numbers.'[4] But she would say that, wouldn't she?

There's no doubt *a* sense in which prison can be *made* to work. One of the crime statistics on which it's safe to rely is that only a negligible proportion of serious offences is committed by people over 65. So if everybody under 65 is incarcerated, the prediction has to be that the crime rate, however defined and calculated, will fall – a prediction which is almost but not quite as spectacularly unhelpful as the prediction that there will be fewer fatalities among rail passengers if the last coach (which is where most fatalities occur) is removed from every train. The typical rejoinder of criminologists and politicians who don't like incarcerating people if they can help it is to say that 'prison is the most expensive means yet devised for making bad people worse'. By this they mean that so little do prisons rehabilitate their inmates, or even deter them from doing the same again, that (as their chosen statistics clearly demonstrate) ex-cons are consistent re-offenders. So where do we go from here? First of all, we need a less ambiguous definition than any politician will ever be likely to give of what is being claimed by the assertion that prison 'works'. Second, we need a set of statistics chosen not because they either bolster or undermine a chosen policy but because they offer genuine comparisons over adequate time-scales. And third, we need some international comparisons which will furnish the nearest we can get to quasi-experimental evidence for the consequences of different decisions on policy. But if we expect agreement then to follow between politicians and their advisers on the Left and their counterparts on the Right, we shall inevitably be disappointed. There is still far too much scope for attitude-peddling based on statistics which, even if reliable (and they won't be), are equally compatible with mutually exclusive explanatory hypotheses.

By this time, some readers are probably wondering why I'm arguing so persuasively against myself. If the statistics on crime in general and the effect of imprisonment in particular are as unsatisfactory, even at their best, as I've been saying, maybe we should stick with the lies and damn lies and leave the statistics out of it. But the correct conclusion is a rather different one. It's that the difficulties which stand in the way of using the statistical techniques available to test presumptively causal hypotheses about 'criminal' behaviour are difficulties in the data to which they're applied. We don't know whether, why, and to what extent poverty increases the probability of crime in the way that we do know whether, why, and to what extent smoking increases the probability of cancer. But we could. The question is insoluble in practice, but not in principle. The difficulties just happen to be more intractable, including not least the impossibility of conducting experiments to whose results the techniques for testing whether correlation amounts to causation could be applied. But there's nothing wrong with the techniques.

Besides, on some topics the data *are* both abundant enough and consistent enough for causal hypotheses to be tested. Murder rates are from this point of view more rewarding than you might expect. Admittedly, there's always scope for argument about the number of 'successful' murders not identified as such, as well as about when a death inflicted by one person on another really *is* 'murder'. But if the same definition of murder is retained over a long enough period and the authorities treat murders as seriously as they generally do, it becomes possible to identify significant trends. The numbers need to be big enough as well as the time period long enough. An anthropologist who learns of two murders in the course of a two-year stint of fieldwork among a society of two thousand people can report a murder rate some five times higher than that for New York in 1994, but you don't need to know all about the ingenious methods which statisticians have devised to test the significance of small numbers to realize that this one would have to be interpreted with very great caution indeed. On the other hand, the British murder statistics are copious and clear and go back a surprising number of centuries; and one of the most striking features of them is a big drop from something like the present-day American rate to something like the present-day British rate from the time at which men no longer carried swords. You can't, admittedly, go straight from there to gun control policy for the USA in the year 2000: although nobody doubts that if weapons are unobtainable there will be a drop in the number of killings with weapons, it doesn't follow that the American gun lobbies are wrong when they say that to ban the sale of weapons would merely drive the market underground. But if, on the other hand, you look at the graph for homicide rates in Britain during the twentieth century you will notice a funny little upwards blip in 1945. Why? One guess is enough. The hard men came back from the Second World War with their army revolvers, and before they handed them in they had one or two scores to settle.[5]

Nobody should have to be reminded that statistical methods are good servants but bad masters. But that proposition is quite often ignored by people who ought to know better. It can't be wrong to squeeze as much information out of a body of data as the appropriate technique makes it possible to do. But it's the ever-present AMs who need watching. Look at the battle which has raged for decades over 'measured intelligence'. The argument is not only about what it is that IQ tests are actually testing but about how much of the variance between different people's scores is to be attributed to heredity and how much to environment. The fact of the matter is that because of the way in which heredity is continuously modified by environment, it isn't possible either to prove or to disprove a claim to the effect that x% of the variance in measured intelligence at any given age is due entirely to the one and the residue entirely to the other. But because of the importance of the issue to educational policy-makers and the moral and political passions which are roused by it, every statistical technique you can think of has been mobilized in the cause of demonstrating that either less or more, as the case may be, of the variance is directly attributable to the different genes with which different people are born.

On the other hand, perhaps it doesn't matter too much that so many people, sociologists included, deploy statistics chosen to support the conclusion they've reached already, since those who disagree with them will have no difficulty in pointing out that that *is* what they're doing. More problematic is the general resistance, to which I've already referred, to thinking in statistical terms at all. The culture of which this book and its readers are alike the products is a supposedly rational and scientific culture. Yet how seldom we think and act that way! Look how many smokers keep puffing away, however many health warnings are given them. Stranger still, look how many high-earning executives and professionals don't take out disability insurance, even though the cost to them is small and the prospective benefit large precisely because their earnings are as high as they are. They say, 'But it isn't going to happen to me', and they're probably right. But only *probably*. And to make matters worse, we're not just unstatistical and self-justifying social animals, but self-satisfied ones. When a million American high-school seniors are asked whether they have above-average leadership ability, what do you think they reply? Over 70% say they do and a mere 2% say they don't. Better still, out of a sample of American university professors, no less than 94% can be found saying that they think they are better at their jobs than their average colleagues![6]

I've not forgotten that I said at the beginning of this chapter that what feels to a successful conqueror like predestination is apt to look to outside observers like luck. But except when having lost a game of skill which they had expected to win, most people don't attribute what happens in the world to luck nearly as often as they should. As Nietszche said, 'No victor believes in chance.' If a large number of investors has been playing the stock market over a period of years, a predictably small proportion of them will make a predictably large amount of money. But unless, like Ivan ('greed is good') Boesky, they've done it by trading on inside information, it's a matter of chance which investors they are. Sure, Warren Buffett, the legendarily successful investor from Omaha, Nebraska, has reasons for what he buys and sells. But so do the investors who sell when he's buying and buy when he's selling. I agree that it isn't *pure* 'luck': since the judgements stock market investors make are more about other investors' judgements of value than judgements about value as such, some may be genuinely more skilful than others. Bridge, like poker, is a game of chance *and* skill. But if stock market investment is more skill than luck, why don't the same pension fund managers come out top of the league table significantly more often than they actually do?

This is a book about sociology, not gambling or pension fund management, and its arguments aren't going to be affected one way or the other by whether Warren Buffett is so rich because he's so smart or thought to be so smart because he's known to be so rich. But serious consideration of the part played by chance in the explanation of human behaviour cannot but help to undermine further the illusion, which sociology and psychology between them have largely dispelled already, that we are the masters of our fates and captains of our souls. Why, to go back to the very beginning, are any of us around at all? The answer given by the primatologists Richard Wrangham and Dale Peterson links the success of the critical tlm which occurred around five million years ago to climate, ecology and diet. But notice how they put it:

> ... the climate has turned. A long drought has settled on the continent. Away from the equator, the tall fruit-bearing trees no longer replace themselves and are outcompeted by dry-country species relying on winds, not animals, to spread their seeds, and so they give little food rewards to fruit eaters. In the dampest areas, where river gullies nestle in protective gorges, a few islands of rainforest provide the last refuges for these apes now surrounded by a spreading ocean of hostile savanna woodland. Eventually, even those little nurturing streams dry up. The loss of rainforest means the loss of food. Breeding will soon cease, and the localized ape populations will succumb, go extinct. It's a common fate for pioneers like these who have spread from their equatorial base to higher latitudes. But pioneers sometimes succeed, and success is what happens to this single group of apes we're thinking about. They are lucky. Something allows their small band to survive and change.[7]

And if that single group hadn't been lucky, I wouldn't have been here to write this sentence and you wouldn't be here to read it.

Now of course Wrangham and Peterson aren't claiming to have *explained* the origin of humanity simply by saying that it was a matter of luck. Its detailed explanation involves contributions from not only primatology but archaeology, anatomy, botany, palaeontology, behavioural ecology and molecular biology. But the card game analogy applies throughout. It's *as if* an enormous pack was being shuffled and dealt, shuffled and dealt, shuffled and dealt; and once 'descent with modification' is under way, some players will stay in the game and some drop out depending on whether the cards fall for or against them. Like it or not, that's the way things have gone on from then until now. It will be no less a matter of luck whether, for example, this book succeeds or fails in competition with the many others which are bidding for your attention. If it does succeed – if, that is, its arguments (its constituent 'memes', if you will) are diffused and replicated among readers who are persuaded by them – that success will no doubt be explicable in hindsight in terms ranging from the marketing strategy of the publishers to the intellectual predispositions of the borrowers or purchasers who are induced to give it a try. But I shall have been lucky, all the same.

VI

Structures and Cultures

I FEEL BOUND to open this chapter with a confession of failure, both individual and collective. For all the well-attested evidence which we (sociologists, that is) have at our disposal about the range of human social behaviour down the ages and across the globe, we have nothing approaching a rigorous and comprehensive system of classification for the different kinds of groups, communities, institutions and societies into which we (human beings, that is) are and have been organized. It's not for want of trying. Human beings have been categorizing their relations with one another for as long as they've had languages in which to do so, and some of the older of these categories have stood the test of time better than some of the newer ones: the distinction between 'monarchic', 'oligarchic' and 'democratic' forms of government, which we owe to the Ancient Greeks, has been and still is more serviceable than the distinction between 'left-wing' and 'right-wing' political parties and regimes which we owe to the accident of the seating arrangements in the French Assembly after the GBE of 1789. But we are nowhere near a taxonomy of human societies comparable to the taxonomy of genera and species with which biologists are able to operate.

The most influential attempt to date is still Marx's. If, as he believed, societies are as they are because of the relationship between what he called their 'forces' and 'social relations' of production, then it follows that there will be as many types of society as can be distinguished from one another in those terms. From that presupposition derive two of the most famous sentences in the literature of sociology: 'In broad outline, we can designate the Asiatic, the ancient, the feudal, and the modern bourgeois modes of production as epochs in the progress of the formation of society. Bourgeois relations of production are the last antagonistic form of the social process of production.' This is Marx in the Preface to his *Contribution to the Critique of Political Economy*,[1] and for all the qualifications and repudiations which have been heaped on it by later sociologists, both Marxist and non-Marxist, it must count as one of the heroic exaggerations on which all nascent sciences initially depend. But it won't do. Quite apart from the inbuilt presupposition that this is a unilinear sequence which will culminate in a supposedly non-antagonistic post-bourgeois mode of production, detailed study by sociologists, anthropologists and historians of the multifarious societies which on this basis would all have to be slotted into one or another of the four pre-socialist modes has blown it apart beyond hope of repair. Four and only four kinds of human societies in the history of the world before 1917? It's a hardly more sophisticated starting-point than the old classification of the elements into earth, air, water and fire.

Yet we are still, however unwillingly, Marx's intellectual legatees. We still refer to the slave societies of Greece and Rome as the 'ancient' world – I've just done it myself in the opening paragraph of this chapter. We all recognize something corresponding to the idea of a 'feudal' society in which arms-bearing landowners extract an economic surplus from subject peasants. We still talk without qualms about 'capitalist' societies and contrast them with the 'socialist' societies which Marx himself didn't live to see. We may not use the term 'Asiatic' any longer, but we still acknowledge the distinctiveness of pre-industrial societies in which a monarchy staffed by a central bureaucracy dominates the local power-holders as well as the peasantry. It may be that we nowadays concede a greater degree of autonomy to both political and ideological roles and institutions than Marx did. But it doesn't stop us from tacitly agreeing that the way in which a society generates and distributes its economic resources is fundamental to any explanation of how it functions and why it has evolved as it has.

This might seem to suggest that there is, after all, something there which we can expand and refine as the course of research may dictate. But for all that there is, as I conceded in Chapter III, a sense in which all of us are Marxists now, modes of production only capture one aspect of the institutional differences between one society and another. To give just one illustration, the well-documented absence of ritual among the hunter-gatherer societies of Africa can't possibly be claimed to be a function of that mode of production for the simple reason that the lives of Australian hunter-gatherers are by contrast full of ritual. Nor does it help as much as you might suppose to supplement mode of production as a criterion with modes of persuasion and coercion. The sad fact is that our current taxonomy of societies is a shambles. To see why, you need look no further than the academic literature in which sociologists and historians have taken issue with each other over the definition of the 'feudal' mode. There is a further irony in this choice of example, since one of the best books ever written about a distinctive set of social institutions is the French medievalist Marc Bloch's *Feudal Society*, published in 1940. But Bloch candidly admits that 'the word feudalism, which was to have so great a future, was very ill-chosen' and that it 'has sometimes been interpreted in ways so different as to be almost contradictory'. He goes on to say that 'the mere existence of the word attests the special quality which men have instinctively recognized in the period which it denotes' and it is indeed that special quality which his own work memorably conveys.[2] But we are left with the same uncertainty as to whether feudalism is a matter of landholding tied to service (the 'fief'), fealty sworn between lords and vassals, fragmentation of political authority, private administration of justice, manorialism, subordination of peasants to lords who hold a monopoly of force, ties of personal dependence, a knightly code of honour, a graded system of property rights, or some particular variant or combination of these. Bloch's own solution was to list a number of such features and add to it the continuing survival of the family and the state – a solution which enabled him to assert with confidence that Japan as well as Europe passed through a 'feudal' stage. But that claim has in turn been disputed just as vigorously as have alternative definitions restricted to Europe, or even to certain parts of Europe, or even to certain parts of Europe for a far more limited period than the period so successfully covered by Bloch.

One way of tackling the problem is to treat concepts like 'feudalism' as what Weber called 'ideal types'. By this he meant that they are logical constructions which provide the standard against which actual instances can be assessed: an ideal-typical 'feudal' society would be one in which all of a chosen set of characteristics such as Bloch's were instantiated in, as it were, pure form. But this solves one difficulty only to create another. It may help to place different societies or regions within them in some notional order of nearer or further approximation to an 'ideal' feudalism. But how are the different components of the ideal type to be weighed against each other? A comprehensive and rigorous classification of societies would enable us to allocate each of them a place in which its distinctive characteristics fitted the label assigned to it without room for argument. But that is just what 'ideal types' *don't* do. 'Feudal', 'capitalist' and 'socialist' aren't terms like 'vertebrate', 'warm-blooded' or 'bipedal'. Nor, even when construed as limiting cases, are they like 'absolute zero' or 'pure vacuum' which stand for extreme values of a measured variable which may not be empirically instantiated but are derived from, and operationalized within, a well-validated theory. The usefulness of Weberian 'ideal types' to sociologists isn't taxonomic at all; it is heuristic, by which I mean that it helps us to pose questions about the relations of different 'feudal', 'capitalist' or 'socialist' practices, roles and institutions to one another in a manner which will (perhaps) generate some illuminating hypotheses about the workings of societies to which these labels can be more or less convincingly applied.

This is where my own confession of failure comes in. In 1989, I published a volume in which I put forward a provisional categorization of human societies which I thought of as an analytic taxonomy rather than a set of ideal types. But it wasn't. As a perceptive reviewer, the medieval historian Chris Wickham, was quick to point out, I had fallen into the very same hole that I thought I had dug myself out of – including proposing a definition of 'feudal' which covered some and excluded other societies on grounds at least as arbitrary as those which enabled Bloch to label Japan a 'feudal' society.[3] I can say, in my defence, that my starting-point was in theory sensible enough. Since there are three and only three forms of power, all societies should be capable of being assigned a place in a notional three-dimensional grid according to their distinctive modes of production, persuasion and coercion. On this basis, it is uncontroversial to say, for example, that the society of which I am myself a member is 'capitalist' (competitive market in labour and goods), 'liberal' (ideology of formal freedom), and 'democratic' (government by parties competing for the votes of a fully enfranchised public). But the problem remains. When it comes to assigning *other* 'capitalist-liberal-democratic' societies places in the notional grid where their similarities to, and differences from, each other will be laid out as rigorously and comprehensively as in the biologists' taxonomy of plant and animal species, we are as helpless as ever.

Nor, I fear, has any sociologist whose writings are known to me succeeded any better than I have. The most popular current

British textbook, Anthony Giddens's *Sociology*, has a page on which is set out a table of 'Types of Human Society', of which there turn out to be seven: Hunting and Gathering Societies, Agrarian Societies, Pastoral Societies, Traditional States or Civilizations, First World Societies, Second World Societies and Third World Societies. But this typology lacks any discernible rationale whatever – it vacillates both between historical and ahistorical criteria and between economic and political institutional forms; and the comments intended to elucidate the distinctiveness of each type only make matters worse. Thus, we are told that Pastoral Societies 'are ruled by chiefs or warrior kings' whereas Agrarian Societies are 'ruled over by chiefs' and Traditional States or Civilizations are 'headed by a king or emperor'. Although industrial societies are not a distinctive type and horticultural societies are ignored altogether, First and Second World Societies are 'industrial' whereas Third World Societies are not; but central planning is a defining characteristic of Second World Societies, even though some Third World Societies are assumed to be centrally planned. Ideology is admitted only by way of the comment that in Second World Societies, 'Major class inequalities exist [as they do both in Traditional States and in First World Societies] although the aim of the Marxist governments of these societies is to create a "classless" system.'[4] Perhaps I'm missing the hidden logic which makes sense of all this. But if so, what is it?

The more encouraging news, however, is that, like the lack of an agreed definition of 'stratification', the lack of an adequate taxonomy doesn't matter as much as you might suppose. It hasn't prevented sociologists and anthropologists (and historians, too) from finding out how all sorts of very different human societies do actually work. You won't find it conveniently summarized in an Encyclopaedia of Comparative Sociology, and still less in a single-authored handbook. Even if Max Weber himself was alive and well, he could do no more than summarize a modest proportion of what is known about the structure and culture of the thousands of human societies documented in the historical and ethnographic record. It can't be done even on so seemingly restricted a category as 'nomadic' societies, as is explicitly conceded by the foremost living expert on pastoral nomadism, A. M. Khazanov.[5] Yet this impossibility is in itself testimony to just how much *is* known about different human societies – 'known' in a sense no less 'scientific' than what is known by primatologists, zoologists and behavioural ecologists about the organization and functioning of the groups, communities, and societies formed by the various social animals which they study from species other than our own.

What's more, for all the differences in theory, method, terminology and political attitude between the various researchers whose conclusions about the human societies which they have studied have withstood attempted disconfirmation by rivals and critics, they almost always provide evidence sufficient for their readers to see how power is distributed and exercised among the society's constituent roles. They may not talk about roles at all, and still less about modes of production, persuasion and coercion (let alone 'systacts'). They may be much more interested in particular economic, ideological or political institutions than in the workings of the society as a whole. Some of them might be aghast at being labelled sociologists rather than anthropologists or historians. But by now we really do know a very great deal about the roles constitutive of institutions and societies from Ancient Greece to twentieth-century China, from the nomadic pastoralists of Central Asia to the Nuer of the Southern Sudan, and from the Maori of New Zealand to the Eskimos of the Canadian Arctic. Whatever uncertainties and disagreements remain – which they do – about matters of detail, and however much scope remains – which it does – for conceptual as well as empirical argument, no would-be general sociologist can plausibly complain that there is not enough reliable information from which testable hypotheses can be derived about how different kinds of societies function and how they have come to be as they are.

Nor is it as if this information is so specific to the particular societies which particular specialists have chosen to study that inter-societal and cross-cultural comparisons and contrasts can't be formulated, even if the specialists themselves have discounted the possibility. Let's go back to 'feudal' institutions and in particular to the practice of vassalage. However 'feudal' is defined, it can readily be demonstrated both that homologous forms of the practice of vassalage have functioned differently in different societies and that analogous functions have been performed in other societies by other practices. Under some environmental conditions, vassalage functioned to augment the power of the vassal's role at the expense of the lord's and under others to augment the power of the lord's role at the expense of the vassal's: a classic illustration is the kingdom of Charlemagne, who was himself aware, as we know from a capitulary of his from the year 806, that the granting of benefices to vassals could work both ways.[6] On the other hand, in Islamic societies in particular, there are to be found other forms of personal commendation and other forms of land-grant whose joint functions were closely analogous to those of the ideal type of the fusion of fiefdom and vassalage as exemplified in Christian Europe. These 'feudal' practices and roles may strike you as of antiquarian rather than contemporary interest: what about the practices defining the roles constitutive of the institutions of modern industrial nation-states? But the same applies in the world of mass parties and trade unions as in the world of fiefs and vassals. Take, for example, the contrast between bureaucratic and clientelistic practices and roles. Bureaucratic practices are not in themselves a product of the evolution of 'modern' societies. Far from it – Ancient Egypt was one of the most bureaucratic societies ever known. But in some present-day societies, personal patronage performs the function that impersonal bureaucratic practices do in others, and does so within their trade unions and their political parties alike. What's more, homologues of patron–client relationships can persist within ostensibly bureaucratic institutions, and homologues of bureaucratic relationships can persist within systems of patronage, even where political legitimacy is, in Weber's term, 'charismatic' – that is, both the source and the agency of the power attaching to the topmost role are personal.

Not the least important conclusion to be drawn from comparisons and contrasts of this kind is that for all the variation in both structure and culture among the multifarious societies in the historical and ethnographic record, it is neither unlimited nor inexplicable. On the contrary: at any given level of population, technology and resources, there are not that many different ways in which economic, ideological and coercive power can be distributed and exercised. As always, the importance of the differences is in the eye of the observer: for all the similarities between the relatively small and simple hunting, foraging and gathering societies in the ethnographic record, the differences between them in not only ritual but technology, part-time division of labour, and relation of co-residence to kinship are, depending on what exactly you want to know, highly significant. But when such societies are compared in terms of the distribution and exercise of power, the overwhelming impression they leave is one of minimal distance in social space between their constituent roles. Resources including food are divided in accordance with a rule of generalized reciprocity, prestige is accorded on a largely personal basis, and the enforcement of discipline and settlement of disputes are carried out without a role to which there attaches a monopoly of the means of coercion. You may find nothing surprising in this: after all, it's much the sort of behaviour to expect among any group of people cast adrift with limited supplies in a small boat on the Pacific Ocean, even if the leader is, as in the actual example of what happened after the mutiny on the *Bounty*, the notoriously autocratic Captain Bligh. But that's my point. However different from one another the individual people who make up a group, community, institution or society of one kind or another, their relationships to one another *in their roles* will conform to practices whose replication their environment will explain.

As societies become larger and more complex, the range of variation in their structure and culture becomes wider, as you would expect. But not that much wider. If you don't believe me, try listing all the ways in which power is, or even could be, distributed and exercised in a large, prosperous, literate, but still pre-industrial society. How many ways can you think of in which such a society's dependent labour force might be organized? There are slavery, serfdom, peonage, wage-labour, forced labour, tenancy, sharecropping, free peasant production, domestic out-work, and ritual exchange between higher- and lower-ranked castes – but what else? Likewise, in the mode of persuasion you can have ranking by age-sets, a ritual hierarchy of purity and pollution, hereditary status-groups graded according to ethnicity, gender, locality, religion or ancestry itself, functional attribution of prestige according to the value conventionally assigned to occupational roles, or a charismatic ranking according to individual personality and achievement – but what else? And in the mode of coercion, you can have mercenaries, professionals, conscripts, a volunteer militia, a servile political and military apparatus, or a decentralization of sovereignty among local magnates and their retainers – but what else? Numerous variations and combinations are possible, and there is as always scope for quibbling about definitions of particular roles. But they are variations and combinations derived from a menu of alternative practices which is far from unmanageably long and far from bafflingly strange.

That is why the parallels between the modes of production, persuasion and coercion of societies far apart in time and place are so often as striking as they are. When the Spanish conquistadors arrived in Central and South America in the early sixteenth century AD, they were confronted with the roles constitutive of societies which had evolved completely independently of their own. But for all the differences by which they were struck in customs, manners and beliefs, they had no difficulty in recognizing economic, ideological and coercive institutions which were in many ways both homologous and analogous to their own. Two large, literate, prosperous agrarian societies which are quite remarkably alike, despite being many hundreds of years and miles apart in time and place, are England in the tenth century AD and Babylonia in the eighteenth century BC. An Anglo-Saxon king, bishop, landowner, merchant, peasant, craftsman, soldier, priest, clerk, tax-collector, schoolteacher, servant or slave would be immediately at home in Hammurapi's Babylonia, and vice versa. In both societies, there were royal and ecclesiastical estates side by side with private landholdings, taxes paid to the king as well as dues to the church or temple, private capitalists engaged in long-distance trade for profit, an active land market, tenancy and serfdom as well as slavery and the possibility of manumission for debt-slaves, written law codes, local agents of royal power liable for military or auxiliary service, administration of justice at village level, and for women, subordinate though they generally were, a right to retain a dowry and bequeath it in due course to a child or children. None of this adds up to some impressively lawlike generalization about how all 'agrarian' societies function. But it does add up to a clear demonstration of the extent to which similar role-maps reflect similar environments and similar selective pressures acting on the practices by which the roles are defined.

Much of the discussion of all this in the literature of sociology revolves around the well-worn concept of 'stratification'. Indeed, there are nearly a hundred English-language books in the Cambridge University Library which have *Social Stratification* in or for a title, half of which are still in print. But since there is, as I remarked in Chapter IV, as little agreement among them on definition of terms as there is among the sociologists or historians who talk about 'feudalism', 'stratification' is in effect no more than a useful metaphor for a social system in which more and less powerful roles are arranged above and below each other in distinct layers – as it might be, upper, middle and lower 'classes', or higher and lower ranked 'castes', or 'age-sets' of dominant elders and subordinate juniors. It presupposes that roles are consistently ranked in the three dimensions of structure which correspond to the three forms of power, so that if we stay with the model of the inverted pyramid each 'stratum' is a triangular plane on which lie the roles belonging to it, like this:

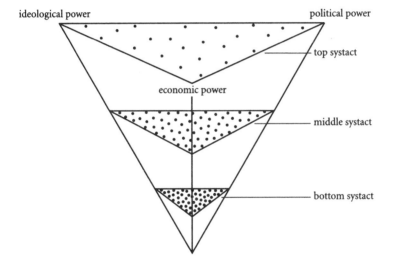

Figure 7

But very few societies on record can actually be fitted to this sort of model. The small and simple societies are, as we have seen, hardly 'stratified' at all, and in the large and complex ones there are so many roles which are inconsistently ranked in the three dimensions and so many people who occupy and perform two or more differently-ranked roles that the society can't be pictured as a stack of even layers without serious distortions and omissions. Worse still, the fact that, as I pointed out at the very beginning of Chapter I, societal boundaries are both fluid and permeable means that the role of, say, a fourteenth-century Norwegian fisherman is 'stratified' not in relation to the central institutions of the Norwegian state with which he has in fact no relationship whatever but to the Hanseatic merchant to whom he annually sells his catch. By all means hold on to the concept of 'social stratification' if you find it helpful. But I suspect that it has retarded the explanation of the distribution and exercise of power both in and between societies of different kinds at least as often as it has advanced it. There are so many different dividing-lines which can be drawn on societal role-maps that sociologists would do better to stop arguing about how many separate layers each society contains and concentrate on identifying the practices whose functions for the roles which carry them explain why power in the society is distributed and exercised as it is.

Matters are made worse, as usual, by the AMs and PMs who are unable to resist the temptation to pontificate about social inequality in general instead of trying to validate well-grounded hypotheses about particular cases. The unsinkable Talcott Parsons, who published two often-cited articles on what he called his 'generalized analytical approach to the theory of social stratification' in 1940 and 1953, topped them up in 1970 with another 56 pages on 'Equality and Inequality in Modern Society, or Social Stratification Revisited' whose first 'crucial point' (his words) is: 'though difficult balances must be held within complex social systems between the imperatives of equality and those of stratification, both sets of imperatives operate in such a wide variety of different respects and contexts that there is no guarantee that they will cohere in a form which is functionally viable for the larger system unless there are mechanisms which are functionally specialized in the relevant modes of integration' and whose concluding sentence is: 'I have suggested that the stability of fiduciary responsibility is to be to a very high degree a function of the actor's capacity to command moral authority, the more so the more stratified in the relevant respects such assumptions of responsibility become.'[7] Thank you for nothing, Professor. Meanwhile, the AMs from Rousseau to Immanuel Wallerstein have been busy marshalling their facts about the distribution and exercise of power in human societies in order to hammer home the message that social inequality is a Bad Thing. Lest the purpose of this paragraph should be misunderstood, let me repeat that sociologists who want to elaborate their own conceptual schemata or propagate their own moral and political attitudes are entirely free to do so. But they are at best a distraction and at worst an embarrassment to those of us who want to explain as best we can why the various human institutions and societies in the world are as they are. What's the point of elaborating a 'generalized analytical approach' which doesn't bring you anywhere nearer to validating one rather than another hypothesis accounting for one or more of the different forms of 'stratification' which sociologists have documented in sufficient detail for the purpose? What's the point of denouncing inequalities in access to or control over the means of production, persuasion or coercion if you haven't established why they aren't either greater or less than they actually are in the different societies in which you are so eager to denounce them?

So far in this chapter, as in earlier ones, I've emphasized the way in which the regularities in social behaviour which hold groups, communities, institutions and societies of different kinds together emerge out of the diverse and conflicting dispositions and temperaments of the people who are their members. There may not be universally applicable laws any more than there are uniformly predictable patterns of human social behaviour. But as soon as you start to concentrate on the functions of a society's constituent roles and the practices which define them rather than the thoughts and feelings of the people who occupy and perform them, you will find goods and services being distributed, criteria of legitimacy and social prestige being upheld, and deviant behaviour being punished or controlled through inducements and sanctions which between them maintain a sufficient degree of stability for labels like 'feudal', 'capitalist', 'democratic', 'authoritarian', and so on, imprecise as they may be, to be plausibly applied to them. Yet for all that the patterns of behaviour are as consistent, the range of variation between them as limited, and the parallels between them across time and place as striking as they are, no sociologist is going to bracket Cambodia with Switzerland, or Rwanda with Sweden. Don't the differences call for explanation as much as, if not more than, the similarities?

Of course they do; and as Weber once said, for the purpose of theory it is a good idea to work with extreme cases. But what makes them 'extreme'? In natural selection, which is more extreme: a shark or a butterfly? In cultural selection, which is more extreme: the beliefs of the Nazis or of the Quakers? In social selection, which is more extreme: the training-schools of the Aztec war-machine from which the young novices emerged to secure the thousands of captives whose hearts would be torn out of their living bodies on the summits of the pyramid temples,[8] or Josiah Warren's anarchic village community of 'Modern Times' on Long Island in which he stipulated that there were to be no delegated powers, no laws or by-laws, and no rules or regulations other than those made by individuals for themselves?[9] Nobody questions that communities and societies can be ranked in terms of any number of selected variables. One of them will have to be the largest, or the most productive per head, or the most extensively literate, or the most egalitarian in income and wealth, or the most complex in terms of kinship structure, or the one with the highest (or lowest) murder or divorce or infant mortality rate, or whatever else may happen to interest you. But that doesn't make it the model against which the others are to be assessed as the backward or deviant exceptions. The sociological pay-off from comparing and contrasting them isn't to hand out medals but to achieve a better understanding of how they all, in their different ways, actually work.

The same applies to the understanding of the spectacular 'run-away effects' which, under certain circumstances, can come about in the course of cultural and social, as of natural, selection. In cultural selection, a striking example is the growing by farmers on the Pacific island of Ponapae of enormous yams (up to 9 feet long!) which consume a wholly disproportionate amount of labour for their nutritional value but function as objects of emulation on account of the farming skills to which they are believed to testify.[10] In social selection, a striking example is the 'winner-take-all' phenomenon, as the American economist Robert H. Frank calls it, which emerges under certain conditions in large, free markets for highly-valued skills. I've chosen this example because your first reaction may well be, as mine was, to see it as just another platitude. Don't we all know about what the American sociologist Robert K. Merton calls the 'Matthew Effect' – the Matthew in question being the author of the Gospel in which Jesus tells the Parable of the Talents ('to him that hath shall be given')? But it's a genuine sociological puzzle whose solution is no less satisfying than, for example, the explanation by the primatologists Charles Janson and Michele Goldsmith of the puzzle that whereas larger primate troops travel further every day to acquire all the food necessary for their members, for some species the proportionate increase in daily travel distance is much higher than for others. (The answer to that puzzle, if you want to know, is to be found in 'cost-of-grouping' theory, from which can be derived the hypothesis, which Janson and Goldsmith's data confirm, that species which normally form relatively small troops will be forced to travel relatively greater daily distances by increased troop size.)[11]

As it happens, I went to hear Robert Frank give a talk at the London School of Economics before I'd read *The Winner-take-all-Society*, and foolishly assumed that he wasn't going to tell me anything I didn't already know. But as I soon realized, the puzzle isn't the 'Matthew Effect' as such but its dramatic emergence in American society on an unprecedented scale. Why, all of a sudden, did the rewards accruing to top executives, baseball players, opera singers, or fiction writers accelerate so spectacularly relative to the rest of the pack? After all, the USA was already a large, free market in which the most successful incumbents of occupational roles like these were just as highly regarded in the 1940s, '50s, and '60s, as in the '70s, '80s and '90s. The answer lies in a combination of changes in the environment of which the most important are the expansion of the consumer market, the improvement in information technology, the reduced marginal cost of production cloning, the increasing pay-off in networking effects of investment in publicity, and not least the awareness of the rewards available to potential competitors for those roles. The result is that it's entirely rational for a large corporation to invest hugely in securing the chief executive, baseball player, opera singer or fiction writer who will be judged, by however slender a margin, the 'best'. The gain in the corporation's profits as market share is won will amply cover the gargantuan salaries, bonuses, advances, stock options and royalties required to outbid other potential employers for the services of Number One.

Notice too that Frank's explanation of 'winner-take-all' markets doesn't appeal to some peculiarity of the American mentality any more than Coleman's explanation of panics and riots appeals to some peculiarity of 'mob psychology'. To explain the peculiarities of American or Balinese or Swedish or Cambodian social behaviour is to demonstrate the functioning of roles which would be similarly performed by any psychologically normal incumbent brought up in that society and recruited into that role. How particular people come to occupy and perform particular roles is a separate question to which natural as well as cultural and social selection is relevant, and to which I shall return in Chapter VIII. But even if, as sometimes happens, some of the roles in the role-map are temporarily vacant, children grow up to perform roles distinctive to their society just as they grow up to speak its distinctive language. Some societies are more complex than others, just as some languages are richer in vocabulary and syntax. But that doesn't make their distinctive structures and cultures anything other than the outcome of a different evolutionary history in which different practices confer different advantages on their carriers because of different features of their environments. It would be as meaningless to assert that American society is either more or less 'normal' than Balinese as to assert that the English language is either more or less 'normal' than Sanskrit. No doubt they will *seem* more or less 'normal' as a function of where the observer comes from. But that's of no relevance whatever to the explanation of them.

Look at Japan. Many of the sociologists who have studied it have done so in terms of an implicit contrast with the United States, and from an American standpoint much Japanese social behaviour, both acquired and imposed, is no doubt 'extreme'. How many readers of this paragraph, I wonder, are aware that in Japan there is an 'untouchable' status-group of *Burakumin* ('special community people'), who are physically indistinguishable from other Japanese but stigmatized because of the ghetto locations in which they, like their families before them, have been born? You may well be surprised to learn about them, and you may well find that you need to be tactful about how you let on to other Japanese that you have. But there's nothing inexplicable about them.[12] There are obvious parallels in the stigmatization not only of

127

the 'untouchable' *Harijan* in the Indian caste system but of the descendants of African slaves in the United States and of the Spanish Muslims who reminded Braudel of them. In the Japanese case, the environment which favoured the practice of stigmatization was one in which certain occupational roles which carried traditionally inferior and ritually segregated status were hereditarily occupied and performed by incumbents confined to prescribed geographical locations; and again there are some interesting parallels from other parts of the world where similar conditions cause stigmatization to become not only self-perpetuating but self-legitimating. To be sure, certain features of the history and sociology of the *Burakumin* are unique to Japan. But so are certain features of the history and sociology of black Americans unique to the United States.

More puzzling in a way, but not therefore inexplicable either, are societies which clearly belong in a common category with numerous others but at the same time have features unique to themselves which not a single one of the others shares. Of this, the classic example is Ancient Sparta – a society about which we know as much as we do precisely because it struck Herodotus, Aristotle, and all the other Greeks, whether they admired or deplored it, as 'extreme'. Sparta was one of many of what the Greeks called *poleis* – a word usually translated into English with questionable accuracy as 'city-states'. Not all Greek societies of the seventh to fourth centuries BC were *poleis*. Some were looser tribal communities or federations which the Greeks called *ethne*. But the *poleis* were, broadly speaking, autonomous, politically centralized, agricultural communities governed by property-owning, arms-bearing male citizens who shared with the citizens of the other *poleis* a common language and culture but preserved for themselves their own distinctive cults, coins and calendars. What was unique to Sparta was that the citizens were wholly uninvolved in agricultural production, which was carried out by unenfranchised 'helots' who were kept under strict control by what we nowadays call 'police-state' methods. There were other peculiarities of the Spartan system as well, including the retention of two hereditary kings reigning jointly, the absence of any urban centre of the kind common to all the other *poleis*, and much more freedom for women than they were allowed in 'democratic' Athens. But it was Sparta's uncompromising militarism which so impressed the other Greeks and which gave rise to a good deal of mythical exaggeration which has to be sifted out from the reliable literary and archaeological evidence which has come down to us.

Even after the sifting has been done, the central institutions through which the practices defining the roles of the citizen *Homoioi* ('Equals') and helots were replicated over successive generations remain remarkable enough. Young males were not only removed from their families at a tender age and brought up in communal barracks but were then forbidden to marry until the age of 30, and the training they underwent was not merely strict but brutal. Yet it worked – not to the extent that the Spartans were never defeated in battle, or never had to suppress an uprising by the helots, or were never confronted by an attempted usurpation of unconstitutional power by one of the *Homoioi* themselves, but to the extent that the practices defining the society's constituent roles were nevertheless replicated virtually unchanged for many generations. When the system broke down, as it eventually did, it was because of a combination of economic and demographic changes: the number of *Homoioi* fell at the same time that the ownership of land became highly concentrated among a relatively smaller proportion of them (or, it might be, of female heiresses). There are many detailed questions about exactly how the system worked which are disputed among the specialists who know most about it, and on some of these – notably the manner and timing of the initial mutations of practices which brought it into being – the necessary evidence is almost certainly irrecoverable. But however extreme, strange, or for that matter repellent you may think it, it was an integrated mode of production, persuasion and coercion no less understandable than the way in which your own or any other society exercises and distributes economic, ideological and coercive power.

The same can be said with equal confidence of any 'extreme case' which could be chosen from the historical and ethnographic record, all the way from the nomadic pastoralists among whom inequality of power is almost non-existent (because dissenters who don't want to do what they're supposed to can simply fold their tents and disappear into the sunset) to despotisms like those of Hitler's Germany or Stalin's Russia where freedom is almost non-existent (because there is a network of informers, intelligence agents and secret police who can at any moment deprive any and all citizens of their livelihood and indeed their lives). That is why the lack of anything approaching an adequate taxonomy of human societies doesn't matter as much as it might. The harder part is the evolutionary part. To show how a society works in terms of its modes of production, persuasion and coercion tells you nothing conclusive about the competitive advantages which its particular practices conferred on the roles which now carry them or the particular features of the environment in which they first appeared that favoured their replication. But that's not a reason to underestimate the enormous amount which we *do* know about the structure and culture of the different societies there are and have been in the world and the analogues and homologues between them.

But what (you may fairly ask) has become in all this of the thoughts and feelings of the people who actually occupy and perform the roles whose defining practices hold the different kinds of society together? By some sociologists, anthropologists and historians, my injunction to concentrate on the roles rather than the people will be construed as not just misguided but offensive. The

British historian E. P. Thompson, in the Preface to his deservedly celebrated *The Making of the English Working Class*, explicitly takes issue with sociologists who talk about 'classes' as things and not relationships. 'Class', says Thompson, 'is defined by men as they live their own history' and 'we cannot understand class until we see it as a social and cultural formation'; and his own aim, as he put it in a memorable and often-quoted sentence, is 'to rescue the poor stockinger, the Luddite cropper, the "obsolete" hand-loom weaver, and even the deluded follower of Joanna Southcott, from the enormous condescension of posterity'.[13] But the two approaches, different though they may be, are not in conflict, any more than, say, the classic reconstruction of the English population back to the sixteenth century by the historical demographers E. A. Wrigley and R. M. Schofield is in contradiction with what social historians have written about how successive generations of English people experienced the changes in family and household composition, birth and death rates, duration of marriages, and percentage of children socially defined as 'illegitimate' which lie behind Wrigley and Schofield's graphs and tables.[14] The apparent conflict between them dissolves as soon as you consider the implications of the distinction which I addressed in Chapter II between the two quite different questions 'why?' and 'what was it like for "them"?'

Nobody can seriously dispute that people are privileged observers of their own behaviour both in the sense of knowing what they are trying to achieve and in the sense of knowing what it feels like to be trying to achieve it. But, as I emphasized in Chapter II, none of us is thereby entitled to claim that we know either why we are trying to do what we are trying to do, rather than something else which we might be but aren't, or how much can be explained about the workings of the society to which we belong in consequence. To rescue the deluded followers of Joanna Southcott from the enormous condescension of posterity involves establishing both what they did believe and what it felt like to believe it, but not to accept without further enquiry their own explanation of their coming to do so. To insist on this is not to disagree with Thompson that 'class' is both a relationship and a 'social and cultural formation' – a proposition already implicit in the definition of the practices defining the roles which sociologists assign to different 'classes' as units of reciprocal action informed by mutually acknowledged meanings and beliefs. But the social and cultural formation within which a given set of 'class' relationships finds expression is at the same time an ongoing structure and culture within which roles are occupied and performed in accordance with institutional rules and the outcome of an antecedent process of interaction between the practices defining those roles and their environment.

In many works of sociology (and of anthropology or history likewise), explanations of why the members of a group, community, institution or society behave as they do are presented side by side with descriptions of their subjective experience of their own and other people's behaviour. But there are also examples of books whose long life on the reading-lists is due much less to the explanation which the author gives of 'their' behaviour than to the author's success in telling it like it was for 'them'. One such is *Caste and Class in a Southern Town* by John Dollard, who spent five months in 1935–6 studying social relationships between white and black Americans in a community to which he gives the fictitious name of 'Southerntown'. Aware as he was of the difficulty of his task, he supplemented his other observations by inviting his black informants to come to a rented office, sit down beside him in a rocking chair, and tell him about their own lives in their own way. The result is a vivid and illuminating picture of what Dollard calls 'the main structure of white–negro adjustment in Southerntown from the standpoint of emotional factors' which has (so far as I am aware) no parallel elsewhere in the academic literature on ethnic relations in the United States. Another classic in the same genre is William F. Whyte's *Street Corner Society*, also written in the 1930s but in this case about a largely Italian-American 'Cornerville' in an Eastern city. Whyte's lucky break, after a series of embarrassing false starts, was to meet up with 'Doc' and his gang ('the Nortons'), whose way of life, relations with the wider community, and internal prestige rankings within the gang he describes as convincingly as Dollard describes black–white relationships in 'Southerntown'. Neither account is solely and exclusively descriptive. Dollard has some now rather dated-looking ideas about the psychological explanation of aggressive and deferential patterns of behaviour between the incumbents of roles unequal in power, and Whyte claims that: 'If we can get to know these people intimately and understand the relations between little guy and little guy, big shot and little guy, and big shot and big shot, then we know how Cornerville society is organized. On the basis of that knowledge it becomes possible to explain people's loyalties and the significance of political and racket activities.'[15] But it's not for that sort of explanation that these two sociology books have acquired and retained their reputations. It's because they enable us to 'know these people intimately' in the way that only novelists are normally able to do.

'Then shouldn't we all read novels instead of sociology books?' No, not instead of – as well as. Remember that I said back in Chapter II that novels *are* sociology to the extent that their authors make them so. If you want to know what it was 'really' like to be one of 'them' among the so-called *gratin* of Parisian society in the so-called *belle époque*, you will get much more from reading Proust's *A la recherche du temps perdu* than even as vivid and illuminating a history book as Barbara Tuchman's *The Proud Tower*. The sociologist Erving Goffman, who although he didn't (so far as I know) ever call himself an 'ethnomethodologist' was an outstanding practitioner of precisely those techniques, goes so far as to say in a footnote that the best accounts yet published on the social dynamics of office parties are to be found in novels by Nigel Balchin and Angus Wilson.[16] But nothing does away with the difference between real people such as sociologists study in their actual roles and fictitious people such as novelists place in invented ones. The test of descriptive sociology, as I have said, is whether honest and self-aware informants agree with the sociologist describing the structure and culture of their society that that *is* what it is (or was) like for 'them'.

The big problems for the descriptive sociologist or anthropologist are what to include and when to stop. This doesn't arise in the same way when you're trying to explain how a group, community, institution or society works, because although the answer to one question raises others in its turn, the first question can still be settled on its own. Did the practice of vassalage strengthen or weaken the power of the kingly role in the time of Charlemagne? (Answer: it weakened it.) Does universal suffrage and a first-past-the-post constituency system function to broaden or narrow the difference between major political parties in a capitalist-liberal-democratic society? (Answer: it narrows it.) Is sharecropping a device which heightens the rate of exploitation of cultivators by landlords? (Answer: Not necessarily. In environments where land is plentiful, landlords tend to be elderly and therefore infirm and young men are able to sell their labour to them on favourable terms; then, as at certain times in certain parts of Africa, it's the other way round.)[17] But to *describe* what the institutions that work this way make life in the societies in question like for 'them', you have somehow, to borrow a phrase of Macaulay's, to 'exhibit such parts of the truth as most nearly to produce the effects of the whole'. The British historian W. L. Burn, in his book *The Age of Equipoise*, has an amusing paragraph about what he calls the 'beguiling' game of 'selective Victorianism' which can, as he says, 'be played for hours by young and old'. What he means is that out of all the abundant documentation available about the lives of the people of Victorian Britain, a whole range of mutually incompatible descriptions can be constructed in accordance with the preconceived notions of the different people constructing them.[18] And so they can. Not only philosophers, preachers and poets, but sociologists, anthropologists, and historians do it all the time. But they don't *have* to. Burn himself shows how it can be avoided – not completely, or conclusively, or (whatever that would mean) perfectly, but in a way which can successfully withstand the accusation of imposing on 'them' a version of their typical experience of their representative roles which is more the author's than their own.

This will probably fail to satisfy those of you who have been persuaded by 'postmodernist' critics that there is no such thing as a criterion of authenticity whereby one sociological description can be said to accord more closely than another with what 'their' experience is 'really' like for them. But I don't believe that any practising sociologist studying people's actual social behaviour in their actual roles in their actual societies subscribes to this view for a moment. Anyone who has seriously tried to understand a community's or society's workings knows perfectly well that some informants are more truthful than others, some of their beliefs more coherent, some of their experiences more representative, and some of their ways of describing those experiences more reliable. It's a palpable *non sequitur* to conclude from the necessary selectiveness of all descriptions that none is less vulnerable to the accusation of self-referential subjectivity than another. The point has nowhere that I know been better put than by the French anthropologist Philippe Descola in the 'Epilogue' to his outstanding study of the Amazonian Achuar, *The Spears of Twilight*, where after freely conceding that anthropologists are 'creators as well as chroniclers' he goes on to say:

But rest assured: I have not imagined the events and characters that provide the material of this story. Each scene truly did take place in the chronological order in which I have narrated it, in the place where I situate it, and with the protagonists whose behaviour I have described. Only their names have been changed so as not to embarrass their descendants in case, with predictable advances in the spread of literacy, they might one day happen to read my book. But on to that measure of truth are grafted two literary effects that anthropologists are bound to exploit, even if they are sometimes loath to admit it: that of composition, which selects from the continuity of lived experience particular clips of action which are reckoned to be more significant than others; and that of generalization, which invests these fragments of individual behaviour with a meaning that can in principle be extended to the entire culture under consideration.[19]

Exactly so. Descola does, I am bound to admit, apply the term 'exotic' to Achuar society, and he convincingly describes *his* subjective experience of the fundamental and often disconcerting differences between the Achuar way of looking at the world and his own. But he goes on to say, just as Herodotus did, that it is this very understanding of how our own illusions relate to those of others that enables us 'to consider them all as legitimate manifestations of the human condition that we all share.'[20]

The ever-present disjunction between the explanation of why people behave as they do in the groups, communities, institutions and societies to which they belong and the description of what it feels like to 'them' to be doing it does not, therefore, constitute an impediment to doing either or both. But it does impose on sociologists, anthropologists and historians alike an obligation to make clear to their readers and themselves where the disjunction lies. Let me stay for a little longer with Descola among the Achuar. When he arrives in their midst, and as he gradually masters their language and integrates himself and his female companion into their domestic and social lives, he sets himself to find out as best he can about their rituals and beliefs, the division of labour and patterns of gift-giving and trade between themselves and others, the prestige ranking of their several roles, their codes and customs of aggression, punishment and retaliation, their sexual standards and mores, their patterns of kinship and affinity, the iconography of their pottery and weaving, their way of bringing up their children, and their attitudes to their social and natural surroundings as they perceive them. He knows better, as his enquiries into their acquired and imposed behaviour proceed, than either to take everything which they tell him at face value or to assume that he knows better than they. He starts to test his provisional explanations of why they do what they do against further observations of their cultural and social behaviour, and at the same time deepens his understanding of their subjective experience by discussing it with them in their own terms. Disjunctions between the two soon begin to emerge, just as they did for Dollard in 'Southerntown' and Whyte in 'Cornerville'. But what is he to do when he is asked by his Achuar friends to spare them a few of his *tsentsak* darts – magical projectiles which shamans secrete in their bodies and use either for putting spells on people or for curing them? He explains to them in embarrassment that his *tsentsak* won't work so far from their place of origin. But the more he protests, the more his interlocutors are convinced that he must not only be a shaman but, since he won't even negotiate over the use of his *tsentsak*, a shaman of a particularly redoubtable kind.

The reader, at this point, is in no doubt that Descola is committed to an avowal that he knows, in a 'scientific' sense of 'know', something about the Achuar way of life that the Achuar don't. Like Evans-Pritchard and Zande beliefs about magic, Herodotus and Neurian beliefs about werewolves, or Dollard and white Southerners' beliefs about the psychology of the 'negro', he at the same time sees it their way and repudiates that way of seeing it. Is he then condescending to the Achuar in the way that Thompson charges posterity with condescending to the followers of Joanna Southcott? No more so than when disagreeing with an anthropological colleague at the *Ecole des Hautes Etudes en Sciences Sociales* about which of two rival hypotheses about the functions of shamanism in Achuar society is better supported by the facts. Is he imposing a Western ideology of science on the Achuar through some form of illegitimate cultural imperialism? No more so than if, when his female companion contracts salpingitis, he saves her life by taking her to the mission hospital for a course of antibiotics rather than to the shaman who claims to have *tsentsak* of the appropriate type. Is he claiming more for his implicit rejection of their conceptual and explanatory framework than his evidence warrants? No more so than when, having listened to the account by one of his informants of a *mesekramprar* (a dream suggestive of impending misfortune), he remains as unconvinced that dreams do genuinely predict future events as he would be if told the same by his own grandmother back in Paris. It doesn't matter how wide a gap may yawn between a sociologist's or anthropologist's explanatory hypothesis about the structure and culture of another society and the understanding which its members have of it themselves. It's true that the disjunction can be brought more clearly into focus when the people under study have, like the Achuar, as little opportunity to learn what 'we' know about physiology and human biology as Herodotus's Neurians. But the issues are no different when the society under study is the sociologist's or anthropologist's own. Neither kind of enquiry is inconsistent with, or at the expense of, the other. Or rather – only if the enquirer is insufficiently aware of the nature of the difference between them. To quote Descola again: 'seeking rational explanations to assuage the feelings of revolt provoked by practices which clash with their own beliefs is the only recourse for anthropologists, who are condemned by the very nature of their task not to set themselves up as censors of those who have given them their trust'[21] – a sentiment from which I am sure that the late Edward Thompson would no more dissent than I do.

VII

History

IN THE DAYS OF MY YOUTH, 'narrative' was a dirty word not
only to sociologists but to many historians as well. It was thought
to imply either the sort of bald recital of events to be found in
the *Anglo-Saxon Chronicle* (723: 'In this year Aethelbald occupied
Somerton and there was an eclipse of the sun.' 724: 'In this year,
the moon looked as if it was suffused with blood and Tatwine and
Bede died'),[1] or else the sort of 1066-and-all-that schoolbooks in
which Kings succeed Kings, the Battle of This follows the Battle
of That, and Top Nations inherit the mantle of greatness from
previous Top Nations. But the reaction against it went too far. As
I remarked in Chapter II, lawlike explanations all presuppose a
narrative of some kind, just as a generalization of some kind is
presupposed by narrative explanations. Moreover, now that the
concept of evolution has re-entered mainstream sociology without
the encumbrance either of outdated 'Historical Materialism' on
the one side or of still more outdated 'Social Darwinism' on the
other, sociology could be said to have become historical by definition. There remains the conventional division of labour whereby
historians trace the detailed sequences of causes and effects which
then inform the comparisons and contrasts drawn by sociologists.
But many more of us are sitting on the same side of the seminar-
table than was so a generation ago, when sociologists and historians
hardly spoke the same language and 'historical sociology' was
treated by many of both as a contradiction in terms.

This is, in a way, a reversion to the same concerns as those which exercised Marx and Weber and their contemporaries. There *is*, after all, *a* sequence which leads from the cultures and societies of early Egypt and Mesopotamia through 'Ancient' Greece and Rome to 'Medieval' Europe and from there to the world-wide 'Expansion of Europe', just as there is *a* sequence from 'primitive' to 'modern' science and technology and *a* sequence in which polytheistic religion precedes Christianity (which in turn precedes Islam). But these aren't privileged sequences in the way that they have too often been taken to be. Not only are European institutions less remarkable than Europeans have generally supposed, but many of their seemingly distinctive features had been anticipated elsewhere: capitalism and the 'rational' techniques and attitudes necessary to it were less of a uniquely Protestant North European phenomenon than Weber was aware.[2] But whatever the detailed history of trade, manufacturing and finance in India or China or Japan, the general conclusion to which it points is the same. The evolutionary process which has made the cultures and societies of the world what they are is not, even in matters of that kind, a unilinear sequence. Confronted with what we know about them all, sociologists have not only to compare and contrast the various sequences with one another, but to identify, if they can, the selective pressures which account for both the differences and the parallels as such. Precisely because our evoked behaviour is a matter of the genes which we have inherited, our acquired behaviour a matter of the bundles of instructions transmitted to us by parents, teachers, peer-group members and role-models, and our imposed behaviour a matter of the practices which have come to define the roles and institutions of the societies to which we belong, no one sequence is inherently more rewarding to study than any others. No one set of practices, roles, and institutions holds the key to the history of mankind, or ever will.

The example with which I propose to illustrate this is Rome –

or, to be more precise, Rome from the mid-second century BC to the time of Julius Caesar's great-nephew Octavian who became, after a protracted series of civil wars, the emperor Augustus. The 'Fall of the Republic', as it is conventionally called, is just as much of a GBE as either the French Revolution of 1789 or the Russian Revolution of 1917, and it has been narrated with style as well as scholarship by successive generations of classical historians who saw themselves as not only its memorialists but its heirs. But to the sociologist, as opposed to the historian, it is a story of a different, although complementary, kind.

Here is a passage from one of the most widely admired of the many books in which the story has been narrated in the traditional manner – the Oxford historian Ronald Syme's *The Roman Revolution*. His title is a little misleading, because it wasn't actually a revolution: it was a transfer of power within the ruling systact, not a usurpation of power from below. But no matter. This is how Syme sets the scene for the rivalry to the death between Gnaeus Pompeius Magnus ('Pompey the Great') and Gaius Julius Caesar:

Pompeius was playing a double game. He hoped to employ the leading *nobiles* to destroy Caesar, whether it came to war or not, in either way gaining the mastery. They were not duped – they knew Pompeius: but they fancied that Pompeius, weakened by the loss of his ally and of popular support, would be in their power at last, amenable to guidance or to be discarded if recalcitrant.

The policy arose from the brain and will of Marcus Cato. His allies, eager to enlist a man of principle on their side, celebrated as integrity what was often conceit or stupidity and mistook craft for sagacity. They might have known better – Cato's stubborn refusal to agree to the land bill for Pompeius' veterans only led to worse evils and a subverting of the constitution. After long strife against the domination of Pompeius, Cato resolved to support a dictatorship, though anxiously shunning the name. Cato's confidence in his own rectitude and insight derived secret strength from the antipathy which he felt for the person and character of Caesar.

The influence and example of Cato spurred on the *nobiles* and accelerated war. Helped by the power, the prestige, and the illicit armies of Pompeius Magnus (stationed already on Italian soil or now being recruited for the government and on the plea of legitimacy), a faction in the Senate worked the constitution against Caesar. The proconsul refused to yield.[3]

The dramatic tale which Syme then goes on to tell is much more than a mere chronicle of events and appraisal of persons. It is also a sequence of postulated causes and effects, in which due significance is given to the institutional context as well as to individual motives and – not least – to luck ('At Brundisium Caesar's heir had again been saved from ruin by the name, the fortune and the veterans of Caesar, the diplomacy of his friends and his own cool resolution. Not to mention chance and the incompetence of his enemies, the accidental death of Fufius Calenus and the fatal error of Salvidienus . . .').[4] But all this is precisely what sociologists studying Rome's evolution from oligarchy to monarchy can take for granted. To them, the question to be answered is: what were the changes in the environment of Rome's republican institutions which lost the advantages to their constituent roles which had previously been conferred on those roles by the practices defining them? Obviously, *some* person or set of persons had to act in such a way as to demonstrate that this was indeed the case before the Republic could be said to have 'fallen'. But to the sociologist, it makes no difference that it was Gaius Julius Caesar who brought it down rather than Gnaeus Pompeius Magnus or any other of the rival warlords whose ambitions and conflicts could not be contained indefinitely within their society's traditional institutions.

The answer to the sociologist's question lies in the previous evolution of Rome's modes of production, persuasion and coercion. From its earliest days, Rome had been a highly militaristic agricultural society dominated by the heads of extended families who occupied the topmost roles and excluded the members of provincial and plebeian families from them. These roles were elective; but the electorate of male citizens was small, venal and easily manipulated. Frequent wars conducted increasingly far outside Italy were interspersed with domestic rebellions, uprisings and conspiracies which were suppressed with equally uncompromising recourse to force. But this meant that more and more able-bodied men were taken off the land for longer and longer periods, with the result that they were increasingly replaced by slaves captured in the wars. At the same time, military commands had to be prolonged for increasing numbers of years beyond the one year for which two consuls serving jointly were traditionally elected. The dominant aristocracy remained, however, as unwilling as before either to concede land reform to the peasantry who manned the legions or to alter the rules under which political offices and military commands were held. This reinforced the long-standing importance of patron–client relationships in Roman society, where the state provided little if any effective redress to the ordinary citizen against intimidation, assault, and even illegal enslavement. Successful generals, whose troops looked to them rather than the state for reward in booty or land, could satisfy their demands only at the expense of their rivals and in opposition to the Senate. Civil war thus became endemic. Only when one warlord had comprehensively defeated the others and thereby transferred the allegiance of his troops to the state itself could stability be restored, just as it was in Japan when the winning warlord, Tokugawa Ieyasu, brought a long period of civil war to an end and imposed a lasting peace in the early seventeenth century AD.

What is surprising (or is it?) is that so far as we can tell, none of the leading figures whose actions can be seen with hindsight to have brought the Roman Republic down had any intention of doing so. The senatorial aristocracy were of course trying to preserve the status quo. But neither the would-be reformers who challenged the Senate over the distribution of land, nor Marius the long-serving non-aristocratic general who for the first time enrolled propertyless men into the legions, nor Sulla the lifelong enemy of Marius who ruled as dictator but retired to die a natural death, nor Pompey who, far from seeking to follow Sulla's example, actually disbanded his army when he returned in triumph from the East, wanted for themselves the role of king. Nor is there any reason to believe that Julius Caesar set out to conquer Gaul with that aim in view. Only when the Senate threatened the lives of the tribunes who supported Caesar, because they opposed its refusal to guarantee his safety by allowing him to stand again for the consulship, did he lead his army across the Rubicon in 49 BC. It's a classic example of the evolution of a society out of one into another mode of the distribution and exercise of power which was neither planned nor foreseen at the time.

To say this is not to belittle the courage, ruthlessness and ambition of Julius Caesar, any more than to diminish the drama of the narrative which leads from his crossing of the Rubicon to his subsequent assassination and his great-nephew's defeat of all other contenders for supreme power. But it's not Caesar's courage, ruthlessness and ambition which explain the fall of the Republic. To argue that would be to fall into what philosophers of science call the 'Genetic Fallacy' of assuming that the cause of an event explains its consequences. 'Why was it Julius Caesar's ambitions which toppled the Republic rather than somebody else's?', intriguing question though it is, can't yield the answer to the question of why his ambitions did actually topple it, any more than 'why was Joe Brady the highest-earning investment banker on Wall Street last year?' yields the answer to the question why winner-take-all markets have evolved as they have in the United States. Roman politicians and generals had been no less courageous, ruthless and ambitious in the second and third centuries BC than in the first. The difference was in the functions of the practices defining their roles in what was by then a significantly different environment.

Sociologists, then, can once again be charged with being more interested in the roles than the people in them. But they perfectly well recognize that the people have to come from somewhere, and that the institutional processes of recruitment and socialization have to be explained too. Not every well-born Roman male was eager for high office and military glory. Ovid, who much preferred amatory and literary to administrative or soldierly activities, explicitly describes himself in one of his poems as 'fleeing from burdensome ambition'. But Roman culture was seriously warlike. Young Romans grew up in the knowledge that war was normal and violence endemic, and if they came from a senatorial family they would be conscious not only of an ancestral tradition of service to the state which they were expected to follow but of the overwhelming prestige accruing to those of them who, having risen to occupy and perform the role of consul, then led a Roman army to victory against its enemies. The 'memes' transmitted by parents and peer-groups all carried the same message: courageous, ambitious and ruthless was what well-born Roman males were brought up to become by imitation and learning alike. The fact that, as in any culture, some were much less receptive to those instructions than others still left an ample supply of wannabes eager to compete for the succession of offices to which public power attached and ready to use whatever means, including assassination as well as bribery, might further their personal aims. As in the case of Winston Churchill in 1940, *somebody* was sooner or later going to come out on top and do the business which was there to be done.

To say so, however, is not a device for smuggling back onto the agenda of sociological explanation some re-engineered new version of the discredited notion of historical inevitability. Roman society didn't *have* to evolve into a monarchy (or, strictly speaking, *re*evolve: it had been a monarchy before it became a republic). But the functions of the practices defining its constituent roles made that outcome more and more likely from the moment that its relentlessly successful expansion by conquest was under way. The story, like every historical narrative, is strewn with might-have-beens. But once the roles of the Roman elite were being occupied and performed in an environment which, as we can see with hind-sight, favoured the continuing replication of the practices defining them, something very unexpected would have had to happen to disrupt or reverse the pattern of social relationships which revolved around patronage, ascriptive status, chattel slavery, military service, and intra- rather than inter-systactic competition for power. Ironi-cally, the *Roman* historians of Rome on whose evidence we depend, like Tacitus and Sallust, didn't see it that way at all. To them, the Fall of the Republic was a matter of personal inadequacies and a collective decline in traditional morality. But if sociology teaches anything, it teaches that historical explanations of that kind aren't explanations at all. Disraeli, who as a successful novelist, as well as a successful Prime Minister, would have disliked almost every-thing in this chapter just as much as any Roman politician or intellectual would have done, famously recommended biography in place of history as giving its readers 'life without theory'.[5] But life without theory is what makes narrative a dirty word.

So not *all* historians are necessarily closet sociologists. But then those who aren't don't explain very much. Or if they do, it's why Caesar won and Pompey lost rather than why the Roman Republic fell.

On the other hand, it would be an obvious exaggeration to claim that explanations of historical events can be validated only if they adhere explicitly to the evolutionary paradigm set out in this book. Indeed, they may even be phrased in 'evolutionary' terms without any implication that they are, or could be, grounded in a recognizably Darwinian notion of 'descent with modification'. When, for example, the Oxford historian J. M. Roberts says in his history of the world that 'the relative ease of simple agriculture in Europe may have had a negative effect on social evolution',[6] he means only that where, unlike in Europe, effective exploitation of the soil required control of irrigation, this in turn required some form of collective social organization. But when, on the other hand, the great Marc Bloch, in *Feudal Society*, says that explanation of multiple fealties in twelfth-century France should be sought 'in the process of evolution which transformed what was formerly a personal property into patrimonial property and an article of commerce',[7] he is pointing directly to the advantages to their carriers of the successive mutations of the practices by which the role of 'vassal' was defined: the vassal who could sell or bequeath his services was in a much stronger position than the one bound by fealty to a single lord. And if you want to know why, to go back to the example touched on in Chapter V, slave-labour rather than wage-labour came to dominate the economies of Ancient Greece and subsequently Rome, you will find that the most convincing explanations suggested by either ancient or modern historians point directly to the advantages to their carriers – in this case, the roles of those who owned or hired the labourers – of the former practice over the latter.

Slavery is another one of those topics of long-standing fascination which has not only generated a huge academic literature but continues to rouse strong moral and political feelings among sociologists and their readers alike. M. I. Finley, the most influential sociologist of Ancient Greece and Rome since Weber, has remarked that ancient historians have tended to be so obsessed with the evils of slavery that they have often failed to recognize the importance of the no less significant and hardly less oppressive practice of debt-bondage, whereby defaulters were compelled to work for their creditors until the debt was repaid – if it ever was. But as always in the sociology of institutions of this kind, the question to be asked is not 'how could the evils of slavery have been allowed to continue unchecked?' but 'why was slavery diffused and its practices replicated rather than other forms of unfree labour such as tied tenants or household dependants or junior kinsmen?' Even in the Roman countryside, where large estates were increasingly worked by slave labour, landowners were aware that free men individually hired on a seasonal basis could sometimes be a better investment. It was a matter of supply and demand. There were not enough free poor available to do the work that had to be done, and the wars of conquest which took so many of them off the land yielded a large supply of captives auctioned off *sub hasta* ('under the spear') in the immediate aftermath of victory. The free poor did, if they survived, return in due course from campaign; but they then expected to resume civilian life either on rural smallholdings allotted to them as deserving veterans or as urban clients of the great houses, not as contractual wage-labourers. Analysis of the process does presuppose a potted history which includes, among other things, the defeat and subsequent destruction of Rome's inveterate enemy Carthage, the Senate's aggressive foreign policy in both the Western and the Eastern Mediterranean, and the successive killings of successive contenders for political power by their opponents and rivals. This is just the sort of narrative which well illustrates the point that for sociologists' purposes potted history is none the worse for being so. You don't need to know the details of the murder of the demagogue Tiberius Gracchus by a gang of cudgel-wielding senators and their retainers headed by one of his own cousins in 133 BC in order to understand why the Republic fell and the part played by slavery in its fall. Given the environment – demographic, ecological and institutional – brought into being in the course of it, slavery was the option which prospective employers of labour in Roman society in the second century BC and thereafter were increasingly likely to choose. The subject is, to quote Finley directly, 'bedevilled by dogma and pseudo-issues, most of them growing out of moral judgements'.[8] But however little the censorious AMs of Roman history may like it, it's another classic example of why the process of social selection selects what it does.

Besides, we must be careful not to fall into the error of supposing that wage-labour is the 'natural' form of employment. However absurd it may seem to us to think of the junior members of the American civil service as the personal property of President Clinton, it seemed perfectly natural to the Romans of the first century AD that their equivalents in the service of the Roman Principate should be slaves of the imperial household, just as it seemed perfectly natural to the members of the Scottish Parliament in 1605 that an employer should be empowered to seize 'maisterful and strong beggars' and 'set his burning iron upon them and retain them as slaves',[9] or to government ministers and officials in the Soviet Union that political prisoners should be worked to what might well be their deaths in the Gulag. Similarly, we may think of slavery in the American South before the Civil War as an aberration from the free-market norm of the expanding, prosperous, democratic North. If so, however, it's sobering to find one leading New England Puritan writing to another in 1645, 'I doe not see how wee can thrive unless wee get into a stock of slaves sufficient to doe all our business', since 'our servants will still desire freedome to plant for themselves, and not stay but for verie great wages.'[10] Nor was wage-labour any more the norm in colonial Hispanic America, where peonage, tenancy, sharecropping and a form of outworking called *repartimiento* were always more widespread, than it was in pre-colonial Africa, where the customary sources of labour were, apart from sharecropping and outworking, slaves, clients, kinsfolk, and even pawns. In Buganda, where European missionaries introduced the practice of wage-payment in the 1880s, they were first told by the native rulers that they ought instead to be buying their workers as slaves, and then told by the workers that it would be quite wrong for them to accept pay from masters to whom they owed tributary labour.[11] Once again, there is an intriguing story to be narrated about when, where and by whom the customary forms of employment were replaced by contractual wage-labour. But it too is a story of the selection of one set of practices instead of another under environmental pressure.

There is another way, too, in which a narrative in terms of the conscious choices of designated people may furnish less of the explanation of a society's evolution than one in terms of the selection of practices in response to designated features of their environment. Practices – like both genes and memes – have a funny way of reasserting themselves. One of the best examples is the Bolivian Revolution of April 1952. This isn't because it's more of an 'extreme case' than the Fall of the Roman Republic or either the French or the Russian Revolutions, whatever that would mean. Nor can it be counted as a GBE in the way that they have to be. Its appropriateness is rather that its unintended consequences followed from a series of events which fitted an almost ideal-typical model of a 'pure' revolution. It didn't, like the French Revolution, emerge out of a revolt against the established institutions of the society from within its dominant systact. Nor did it, like the Russian Revolution, emerge from below in response to the failure of the dominant systact to prosecute successfully a national war. It was a spontaneous overthrow by violence of the government in power by a classic coalition of bourgeois radicals and proletarian mineworkers with peasant support under the leadership of a revolutionary political party. After it, the army was purged, the big mining companies were nationalized and the mines jointly administered with workers' representatives, civilian militias took over control of the means of coercion, devaluation of the currency wiped out the value of the rentiers' assets, and the *hacienda* lands were handed over to the peasantry. But what then?

The unintended consequences were several, including not least an increased rather than diminished dependence on the United States and a return to authoritarian government under General Barrientos after a not quite bloodless military coup in November 1964. But the most interesting consequence, for the purposes of this chapter, is what happened in the countryside. As the Aymara *campesinos* of the Yungas region told the American anthropologist Dwight Heath,[12] 'now we are becoming human beings!' And no wonder that was how they felt. The land was now theirs, the vote was now theirs, and the labour services which they formerly owed to the *hacendados* had been abolished along with their ascribed status as *indios* inferior by birth. Decisions formerly taken about local disputes by the *hacendados* were now taken by *sindicatos* of which the newly-enfranchised *campesinos* were all equal members, and the former *hacendados* mostly moved off the land altogether into the towns. But it would be a serious mistake to suppose that the pattern of social relationships had been transformed. Here are Heath's conclusions in his own words:

1. The patron–client type of functional relationship has been reconstituted in a new form in which the syndicate (or sometimes its secretary-general) assumes the dominant paternalistic status formerly held by the hacendados and the ex-colono occupies a relatively dependent and servile status.

2. At the same time, it is noteworthy that, for certain limited purposes, ex-colonos are happy to retain the old patron–client relationship that linked them as dependents of specific ex-hacendados, despite their resentment of years of 'slavery' and their rallying slogan of 'class warfare'.

At first, as in both the French and the Russian revolutions, the peasantry wanted just to be left alone to cultivate their plots as their own. But when the time came for them to market their surplus produce and to deal with the authorities located in the towns, they turned to the ex-*hacendados* who had the necessary experience and skills to act as brokers or middlemen on their behalf and re-established traditional ties of *compadrazgo* (co-parenthood) with them. Conversely, when the secretary-generals of the *sindicatos* came to exercise the local judicial and administrative functions which the *hacendados* used to do, they expected the wives of the former *colonos* to cook and serve their meals for them just as they had had to do for the old *hacendados*.

This is only one of all sorts of different ways in which practices whose environment might seem to have turned against them can re-emerge, recombine, mutate or be diffused across both social and geographical space with what may be unexpectedly long-lasting effects on the society's role-map. There are no convenient generalizations. Just as in natural selection biologists have to go and find out at first hand precisely what has favoured one set of genes carried by one set of interacting organisms rather than another, and in cultural selection anthropologists have to go and find out at first hand precisely what has favoured one set of memes carried by one set of informants' minds rather than another, so in social selection do sociologists have to go and explore the records of events and states of affairs which historians, anthropologists or archaeologists (or sometimes they themselves) have assembled in order to find out precisely what has favoured one set of practices carried by one set of interacting roles rather than another. None of these aims are in conflict with each other, any more than are either the methods or the results of historians as opposed to sociologists. But there are a few crude maxims which sociologists will on the whole be well advised to follow. First: don't listen to the rhetoric, look at the roles. Second: don't stay with the people, follow the practices. And third: don't get hung up on who did what when to whom, but spot what it is in the environment in which they did it that explains why they did it as they did.

Since a society's evolution out of one mode of production, persuasion or coercion into another can only be explained with the benefit of a large dose of hindsight, the disjunction between the explanation of why it happened and the description of what it felt like to 'them' is bound to be even greater than that between the explanation of its workings within a previously stable structure and culture and 'their' subjective experience of those workings. What's more, the people who are best placed, by virtue of their roles, to understand how their society works are often those most likely to be wrong about why it changes (or doesn't). This isn't just because (as I remarked in Chapter IV) they often have rather unrealistic views about the people in roles less powerful than their own, or even because (as I remarked in Chapter II) they often have rather inflated views about their own abilities and achievements. It's because the experience of the exercise of power is an inherently misleading one. To the sociologist, the decisions of powerful people may be random inputs into the ongoing processes of cultural and social selection. But try telling that to Julius Caesar or Chingiz Khan! You can hardly expect the thrusting politicians, rapacious tycoons or charismatic leaders of ideological crusades to think of themselves as random inputs. 'I'm not a random input, I'm a hero!' It's not that they don't accept that purposive actions, even their own, can have unintended consequences. It's that to *them*, their purposes are the driving forces and the people and things which so annoyingly frustrate them are the random inputs, not the other way round.

The sociologist who claims that it *is* the other way round isn't thereby denying that people in powerful roles don't sometimes achieve their aims and that the future evolution of their societies may be altered as a result. But, as I pointed out in Chapter I, to identify the power-holders' motives still leaves their motives to be explained; and even then, the explanation of their motives won't provide the explanation of why their actions resulted, if they did, in changes to the institutions of their societies which accorded, if they did, with their aims. Successful reformers or revolutionists haven't explained their success unless and until they have done for themselves what the sociologists studying the workings and evolution of their societies will do subsequently – that is, put forward genetic, motivational *and* functional hypotheses which between them fit the evidence better than any plausible alternatives. They may still be entitled to claim to have been shrewder and more far-sighted than their opponents and rivals, just as Warren Buffett is entitled to claim to have been shrewder and more far-sighted than the other investors who sold when he was buying and bought when he was selling. I'm not denying that Caesar was a more able politician than Pompey, or Bismarck than the hapless Louis Napoleon whom he so comprehensively defeated in the Franco-Prussian war of 1870–71. (How can one not doff the cap to the politician who said, 'Believe nothing until it has been officially denied'?) But that doesn't explain their success. To say that their ability explains their success and then cite their success as proof of their ability would be equivalent to the vacuous claim that fitness is the explanation of survival and survival the proof of fitness.

Bismarck, to be sure, was just as keenly aware as any latter-day sociologist of the unintended consequences of purposive social action. That's why he made it a rule of policy always to keep his options open until the last possible minute. But in doing so, he demonstrates the very point which I'm concerned to make: the shrewd politician is the one who recognizes, as the latter-day sociologist does, that the course of historical events is only ever explicable with hindsight. Bismarck remains the unifier of Germany, but not because he knew in advance how the unification was going to come about. It's the same point as Karl Popper's about the impossibility of a predictive sociology. The shrewdest politician in the world, even if (or because of) occupying a role to which there attaches the capacity to influence future events, can no more provide in advance the explanation of the still imponderable outcome of that influence than can even the most knowledgeable sociologist. This isn't to deny that contemporaries can see for themselves that their society is going through a period of change which, whatever the new order turns out to be, makes the old one irrecoverable. No members of Russian society after the GBE of 1917 needed a professor of sociology to make them realize that the evolution of their society was taking a new and in some ways irreversible turn. But the disjunction between what it felt like at the time and how it was to be explained with hindsight was as acute for Lenin himself as it was for any of the Russian people over whom he had so improbably come to have dictatorial power.

In order to see just how wide the disjunction can be in even relatively 'normal' times, there is no need for British sociologists to look any further afield than their own society during their own and their parents' lifetimes. If any two British prime ministers of the twentieth century qualify for heroic status, they are presumably David Lloyd George and Winston Churchill. But the institutions of British society evolved as they did as much in spite of as because of them. Lloyd George wanted above all else to keep a Liberal–Conservative coalition intact after the First World War with himself as its head, but it fell irrecoverably apart. Churchill wanted above all else to keep the British Empire intact after the Second World War, but it fell irrecoverably apart too. Lloyd George failed to effect social reforms on which he had claimed to be set, while Churchill failed to dismantle social reforms to which he had claimed to be opposed. Both came to power when only a short time before nobody would have expected it, and fell from power when only a short time before everybody had thought them secure. Careers like theirs, it might be said, merely illustrate the part played by luck in the ups and downs of party-political life. But as soon as you start to examine in detail the actual changes which took place in Britain's economic, ideological and political institutions after 1918, you will find that neither government ministers nor their officials had any real idea of the selective pressures which a changed environment was imposing on the practices by which the role-map of British society was defined.

Let me cite just two examples. One of the most striking social trends over the period is in the field of housing: what had been an overwhelming preponderance of private rented housing turned into an overwhelming preponderance of owner-occupation.[13] Nobody planned it. The tlm that started it all off was the introduction of rent control in 1915, which was intended as a purely short-term measure. But the housing shortage which followed the ending of the First World War meant that if rent control was removed, the government's popularity with the now enlarged working-class electorate would nosedive. So it was left in place. But that meant that landlords started to look for other investments, while the building societies, to which increasing amounts of money were accordingly being lent, had no outlet for it other than business generated by transfers of property from rent into owner-occupancy. Meanwhile, the incomes of those in work were starting to rise and building costs to fall, resulting in a boom in housebuilding for private sale. Private landlords could neither match what the building societies were offering nor secure an adequate return on their capital if they did, while owner-occupancy was now within the reach of the best-paid manual, as well as all but the worst-paid non-manual workers. After the Second World War, both Labour and Conservative politicians encouraged local councils to build housing for rent, which they did. But as real incomes continued to rise, the mortgage relief available to income-tax payers became relevant to an increasing proportion of working-class households, while ownership became steadily more attractive to tenants who at the same time were increasingly dissatisfied with the services offered to them by the local authorities as their landlords. The final irony in this particular piece of potted history is that when Margaret Thatcher's government sought to recreate a market in privately rented housing, the fall in housing subsidies caused the costs of housing benefits to rise, thereby increasing the very 'welfare dependency' which she wanted to reduce.

Hardly less anomalous is the story of unemployment benefit itself. At the end of the First World War, ministers and their officials had been braced for a rise in unemployment as the demobilized veterans re-entered the labour market. But it didn't happen. On the contrary, there was a roaring boom. But the boom then collapsed – so much so that towns which had previously been strongholds of the so-called 'staple' export industries found nearly half their insured workers jobless. The government's response was predictably hesitant and confused, but in 1921 a limited concession (as it was thought to be) was made whereby certain categories of the unemployed could draw 'uncovenanted' benefit – i.e., not covered by unemployment insurance contributions. The idea, or rather the fiction, was that such payments were merely an advance on future insurance contributions. But the principle once breached was never restored. The mutation turned out to be critical, and its replication assured. From there, the story goes on both to increasing hand-outs of public money and to increasing attempts to limit them – eligibility criteria, means tests, and far from wholly effective measures for the prevention and detection of fraud. The means test itself became a high-profile political issue, and when it was abolished in 1941 Labour politicians, in particular, took it to be dead and buried. But so far was this from being the case that by the 1990s over a third of British households had one or more members drawing a means-tested form of support, and that after more than a decade of 'Thatcherite' government.

In case this sounds too cynical, let me emphasize that I am not saying that all politicians are deluded incompetents. Nor am I saying that they should be replaced (God forbid!) by sociologists. But those most likely to establish and preserve a reputation for wisdom are those who recognize just how much their success in doing so depends on things and people other than themselves. Richard Dawkins, in the Preface to *The Selfish Gene*, describes his continuing astonishment at the inescapable biological truth that we are all survival machines blindly programmed to preserve the genes of which we are the carriers. I agree, but would add that I feel an equal, and likewise continuing, astonishment that we are all survival machines with minds programmed to exchange with one another the memes which we carry as members of our common culture and to interact with one another as the incumbents and performers of the roles defined by the practices which we carry as members of the societies of which our roles are made. If, in consequence, the course of human history comes to seem more a matter of chance, and less a matter of choice, than it is comfortable to believe, that doesn't make the study of either biology or sociology any less exciting. Far from it. When Dawkins says, 'I have long felt that biology ought to seem as exciting as a mystery story, because a mystery story is what biology is', I merely want to add: 'and sociology too'.

VIII

Ups and Downs

I HAVE BEEN INSISTING since Chapter I that human societies are made of roles and the practices defining them, and that roles and the power attaching to them are what sociologists study. But people don't always occupy and perform the same roles all their lives. Nor do they always occupy and perform roles located similarly to those their parents did when they were born, or when they entered their first adult role. It's true that in some societies there is very little movement of this kind: the children of slaves are slaves, sons follow their fathers' trades, political power is vested in successive descendants of the same ruling families, intermarriage is within the same tightly-defined status-groups, education is segregated according to the inherited rank into which the child is born, and intellectual or priestly roles are more or less hereditary. But there are no societies in which nobody ever moves out of one role into a higher- or lower-ranked one and no role ever changes its location relative to others in social space. This is what sociologists are talking about when they use the term 'social mobility': *individual* social mobility is movement of persons between roles, and *collective* mobility movement of roles themselves – a distinction which needs then to be refined by introducing the further one between *inter*-generational and *intra*-generational mobility.

The topic is of such obvious sociological interest that it's surprising how long it has taken sociologists to start studying it systematically. In nineteenth- and early twentieth-century Britain, long before any reliable statistics had been collected, it was a topic of intense interest not only to academic observers but to ambitious men and women at all social levels who hoped to rise or feared to fall and were as familiar with the legend of Dick Whittington as they were with the edifying stories of high achievement from humble origins set out in Samuel Smiles's best-selling *Self-Help* and *Lives of the Engineers*. But it was only in the middle of the twentieth century that rigorous analysis of rates of individual social mobility based on statistically adequate samples of national populations began to be carried out.

Some of the techniques which sociologists have by now developed for that purpose are quite fancy. But the basic method is one which requires nothing more than simple arithmetic. The starting-point is a table with two columns and two rows. The adult population of the society under study is distributed among the four cells of the table in accordance with their own roles (categorized as either high-ranking or low-ranking) and the roles of their parents at the time of their birth. Assume, to start off with, that occupational roles are taken as the indicator of rank and classified either 'middle-class' or 'working-class', and the sample drawn only from males. The 'mobility table' will then look like Figure 8 (overleaf):

The fun begins when you put some numbers into the cells, whether as guesstimates of the actual rate of movement between fathers' and sons' generations in your own (or any other) society or as hypothetical alternatives somewhere between the theoretical minimum (b and c are both zero) and the theoretical maximum (a and d are both zero). The assumption that occupational roles can be neatly divided in this way, even in twentieth-century industrial societies with a free labour market like Britain or the United States, is of course an oversimplification, as is the exclusion of women. But let's go ahead and demonstrate how 'open' a society Britain

		SON'S RANK		
		middle class	working class	
FATHER'S RANK	middle class	a	b	$a + b$
	working class	c	d	$c + d$
		$a + c$	$b + d$	*total*

Figure 8

is by assigning a number to c. It turns out that for Britain (or, strictly, England and Wales) in the 1970s, it was in fact a number equivalent to about a third of all the men who had been born into the working class – higher than Spain, lower than Sweden, but high enough by any standard to dispel the notion of a castelike society where a boy born into a working-class family would be fated to spend his life in a working-class job like his dad's. Notice that the value of c as a percentage of $c + d$, and likewise that of b as a percentage of $b + d$, depends on what those totals are – in other words, on the relative size of the middle and working classes in the different generations; and if the relative number of middle-class roles has grown (which it has), the extent to which $a + c$ is a higher proportion of the total than $a + b$ will directly affect the value of c. Notice also that a may depend on differential fertility

– that is, on whether middle-class fathers actually had enough sons to fill the middle-class roles available – and that c may be a very different percentage of $a + c$ than of $c + d$. But it's still a matter of simple arithmetic, and it's always, at the very least, suggestive to compare the rates of movement between different generations both between one society and another and between the same society at different times.

There are, admittedly, some further complications. For a start, the sociologist's informants may be misreporting their father's occupations at the time of their birth; and even if they aren't, $a + b$ and $c + d$ can't be an accurate representation of the distribution of the male workforce as it ever was in any actual year because of all the different birth-dates of the sons. Moreover, allowance needs to be made for *intra*-generational mobility. The fathers may have been on their way to a higher- or lower-ranked role in the year of their sons' births, and the sons may be on their way to a higher- or lower-ranked one in the year that the study is being done. Nor is it really plausible to divide all occupational roles between two 'classes' only: there are many which are either borderline or inter-mediate, and there is a small but very significant minority of 'elite' roles which belong in a category of their own at the top, as well as a shifting category of people at the bottom who have no jobs at all. But as soon as the sample is subdivided into not just two systacts but three or more, the calculation of mobility rates becomes far more sensitive to arbitrary decisions as to where the lines should be drawn and therefore to the number of roles in the different cells of the tables and consequently the rate of both upward and downward mobility. When women as well as men are included, something has to be done with the housewives who have no inde-pendent occupational roles of their own. And if international com-parisons are to be made, some means will have to be found by which mobility rates in capitalist industrial societies are assessed relative to mobility rates in socialist industrial societies where the 'working-class' person may be a relatively well-paid worker 'by hand' enjoying the privileges and opportunities that go with membership of the ruling political party, and the 'middle-class' person a relatively poorly-paid, insecurely-employed worker 'by brain' denied opportunity for advancement on account of 'bourgeois' origins.

You may by now be thinking that, in view of all this, calculation of mobility rates must in practice be a waste of research grant money, computing equipment and sociologists' time. But it's not. As with the lack of an adequate taxonomy of human societies, the problems aren't as serious as they at first appear. The sociologists at the forefront of research into social mobility are perfectly well aware of all these difficulties and have a number of techniques for dealing with them. In the British case, the most valuable study to date is the work of a team at Nuffield College, Oxford, under the sociologist John Goldthorpe whose sample of men aged between 25 and 64 in 1972, distributed among seven categories of occupational roles, has provided the data from which, when supplemented by data from other sources on women's mobility and on recruitment into the very small number of 'elite' roles at the very top of the occupational hierarchy, a number of interesting conclusions can be, and have been, drawn.

That third of working-class sons who have risen into middle-class jobs turns out to be an excellent starting-point. So far as men's careers are concerned, it means that there is indeed a substantially greater number of vacant middle-class roles than are filled by the sons of middle-class fathers. There is, as you would expect, some downward mobility by middle-class sons into working-class jobs (although virtually none by sons of elite fathers), but some of it is short-term only. Indeed there is quite a lot of intra-generational mobility both ways between middle-class and working-class roles, some of it by men who cross the line more than once in the course of their careers. But the majority of working-class sons still remain in working-class jobs throughout their careers, and their chances of rising into elite roles are very small indeed. Although more men in elite roles were born outside the elite than within it, the Oxford sociologist Anthony Heath has calculated that a man from a working-class home has about one chance in 1,500 of getting into *Who's Who* as compared with one chance in five for a man born into the elite.[1] When the mobility patterns of women are included, the picture is complicated by those who move upwards (or, less often, downwards) through marriage rather than career. But those with full-time careers (who, since genuine two-career families are relatively rare, are more often single) have higher rates of downward mobility and less favourable chances of upward mobility than men do; and since women are much more likely to be temporary or part-time members of the labour force than men are, it is true to say that in terms of occupational roles the opportunities for upward mobility available for men are to some extent at the expense of those for women.

These calculations, for all the technical difficulties which they raise and unsolved problems which they pose, are reliable enough to dispel a number of preconceptions about the 'openness' or otherwise of British society; and the same holds for other present-day industrial capitalist societies where studies along similar lines have been carried out. Even the most open are characterized, statistically speaking, by significant inequalities of opportunity, but not even the least open prevent significant movement across the dividing-lines separating 'middle-class' from 'working-class' roles and 'elite' roles from the rest. It's only if you then want to know what determines who, individually speaking, rises or falls either inter- or intra-generationally, that you will find it much more difficult to get conclusive answers. This is another of the topics on which the relationship between individual psychology and aggregate social behaviour is both complex and elusive. Education is obviously important in qualifying some people rather than others for more rewarding, prestigious and influential occupations. But when the relation of education to social mobility is systematically studied, it's striking how little it actually explains. The assumption of many would-be reformers that greater equality in educational performance would result in greater equality of opportunity for entry into higher-ranked occupational roles is not borne out by the facts. Education does help you to start your career in a better job and it helps your chances of promotion thereafter. But when the sociologists get down to measuring the relative influence of education as such on people's chances of upward mobility, it turns out to be swamped by the effects of other variables, known and unknown. Perhaps we shouldn't be surprised. After all, we can all think of any number of influences other than education on our own and other people's careers, from burning ambition sustained against all the odds to a chance meeting with a casual acquaintance whose personal recommendation tilts the scale. Natural, cultural and social selection are all involved. Your genes affect your potential to be a professional basketball player or a professor of physics or a concert pianist. Your peer-group furnishes you with role-models to be imitated, tastes to be adopted, and ideas to be pursued. The institutions of your society may discriminate against you if you are female or black, work in your favour by expanding the number of roles you happen to be qualified to fill, or take the matter out of your hands altogether by conscripting you into the army when you thought you were going to law school. I don't decry the value of the studies of personality, upbringing, sibling relationships, schooling and interpersonal influence which all have a bearing on who gets where and how they get there. But the most valuable lesson that the studies of social mobility have taught us is the importance of the purely arithmetical influences which mean that, on the one hand, all sorts of people will *have* to be on the move from role to role while, on the other, there is only scope for far fewer of them to do so than may be just as well qualified and highly motivated as those who succeed.

It may sound as if social mobility can profitably be studied only in present-day societies where the necessary data are obtainable and the appropriate techniques can be brought to bear. But although I've used for illustration my own society in my own lifetime, a surprising amount can confidently be asserted about social mobility rates at other times and places. We can't of course reconstruct the sort of 2 × 2, let alone 7 × 7, tables which we can construct for contemporary Britain or the United States or Sweden or Spain. But we can make some pretty good guesses about, for example, rates of manumission of slaves in Ancient Rome and about the proportion of the senatorial nobility who were or weren't the sons of senators themselves. More remarkably, the sources exist which make it possible to compare the proportion of consuls under the Roman Principate who were the sons, grandsons or great-grandsons of consuls with the proportion of successful candidates for the early Chinese civil service of the twelfth and thirteenth centuries A D who were the sons, grandsons or great-grandsons of civil servants. The answer turns out to be 33% in the first case and a not very dissimilar 40% in the second.[2] And the Roman literary sources have also preserved for us some good anec-dotal examples of spectacular long-range upward mobility, includ-ing a slave beautician who somehow rose to be a consul and provincial governor, who testify at once to its desirability and to its rarity, then as now.

There is, to be sure, a danger of over-interpreting the fragmen-tary evidence for mobility rates which survives from societies long past. But mobility rates are a significant aspect of the way in which power is distributed and exercised in societies of any and all kinds. To calculate them, where and when it can be done, is not just to discover something illuminating about how the society functions and why it has evolved as it has; it is also, like so much other sociology, to discover something about the frequently misleading ways in which contemporaries portray their societies to themselves and one another. There is a fascinating example from Marc Bloch's world of 'feudal' France. Contemporaries (and therefore later historians, including Bloch himself) believed that access to the nobility had been relatively open in the ninth and tenth centuries but became much more restricted after about the year 1000. But since Bloch wrote his famous book, detailed examination of the witness-lists of the surviving legal documents of the period has been carried out which shows the opposite. The French nobility of the period was in fact *older* than it represented itself as being: as so often, an ideology of the present was being projected on to the reality of the past.[3]

Individual mobility, however, is 'upwards' or 'downwards' if and only if there attaches to the roles between which rates of mobility are calculated more or less economic, ideological and/or coercive power. In a capitalist industrial society where middle-class people were no better off, economically speaking, than working-class people, both were accorded equal social prestige, and neither enjoyed more or less political influence than the other, movement in social space between 'middle-class' and 'working-class' roles would be of no more sociological significance than the proportion of doctors' sons and daughters choosing to be lawyers rather than doctors or lawyers' sons and daughters choosing to be doctors rather than lawyers. Such a society hasn't happened yet. But there can be no doubt that in the role-map of British society as it has evolved over the last hundred years the social distance between 'middle-class' and 'working-class' roles has narrowed and that this pattern of collective mobility tells us as much or more about the distribution and exercise of power in British society than the fact that the growth in the number of middle-class roles has drawn an increasing proportion of sons and daughters of working-class families into 'non-manual' employment.

The best way to see this is to imagine yourself the son of a British working-class family who entered the labour market as an unskilled labourer in the 1880s. Throughout your early adulthood you would have had a succession of more or less casual jobs paying less than would enable you to support a wife and two children on an adequate diet; you would have been looked down on, socially speaking, not only by your employers and your starch-collared male contemporaries in the ledger offices or behind the shop counters but by the skilled artisans owning the tools of their trade and even by the semi-skilled, machine-minding 'operatives' on the factory floor; and you would have been ineligible to vote at general elections even after the Reform Bill passed in 1884. But you would live to see your wage-rate raised well above Seebohm Rowntree's 'poverty-line', your and your family's entitlement to welfare benefits enormously enhanced, your style of life much more closely assimilated to that of middle-class families, your trade union representatives accorded recognition on near-equal terms not only by the labour movement but even by the governing elite, yourself and your adult female relatives all enfranchised, and a political party formed explicitly to represent the working-class interest not only displacing the Liberal Party of your youth but winning an overall parliamentary majority in 1945. You might think that these changes still left much to be desired. But you could hardly think that they didn't reflect a significant change in the distribution of power in British society.

There is, however, a set of circumstances under which collective mobility becomes even more important, and that is when individual upward mobility is simply not possible – or, if possible, ideologically illegitimate. If you are a Japanese *Buraku* whose place of birth is held on file by the Osaka police, or a villager in Hindu India locked into your designated 'sub-caste' (*jati*), or a black

American in Dollard's 'Southerntown', or a Jew in Hitler's Germany, there is no way up unless you can somehow conceal your origins by 'passing'. There are all sorts of permutations on this. People born with one skin colour can't exchange it for another. But people can sometimes conceal or falsify their family background, or change their names, or learn a new language or dialect or accent, or adopt a life-style which will secure their admission into a status-group from which they are in theory (and even perhaps by law) excluded. Even the *Burakumin* can do it, albeit with considerable difficulty and inconvenience, by going through a complicated legal procedure to change their *honseki* or 'place of registry' (but since the previous address is recorded, they have to do it twice before they can pass as 'ordinary' Japanese). In Ancient Rome, slaves sometimes succeeded in passing as free, non-citizens as citizens, freedmen as equestrians, and Egyptians (whom the Romans regarded as of inherently low status) as Greeks;[4] in medieval Europe, dependent tenants sometimes succeeded in representing themselves as freeholders; and in early Islamic societies, converts to Islam sometimes avoided discrimination at the hands of Muslims born in the faith by inventing fictitious genealogies for themselves. Or individual mobility can be achieved over more than one generation, as by the sons or grandsons of a bourgeois who had purchased office in pre-Revolutionary France, or by the son or grandson of a Peruvian of Indian birth who is able to pass as a *mestizo*. But only if the roles themselves come together at the same systactic level in social space will genuine equality between person and person be achieved.

There are many examples in the historical and ethnographic record of just such a collective narrowing of social distance. It may be between women and men, or black people and white people, or old lineages and new, or lower-ranked castes and higher-ranked castes, as well as between 'working' and 'middle' classes in the way that I have just described in the case of Britain. Once again, it would be a mistake to suppose that there is a uniform trend. Under some conditions, a mutation of practices in the ideological dimension of the distribution of power will be replicated and diffused to the point that significant collective mobility will be achieved by the lower-ranked roles. But the new role-map will be stable only if the same environmental conditions continue to hold. And human beings the world over are, like it or not, extraordinarily quick to stigmatize what sociologists call 'out-groups' on what to the uninvolved observer may seem both arbitrary and trivial grounds. In Chapter II, I gave as an example of the sort of question typically asked by the members of one culture about the members of another, 'How can they bear to eat their meat raw?' But in Herodotus's culture, and likewise Confucius's, people who were alleged to eat their meat raw were defined not merely as different but as self-evidently inferior – uncivilized, backward, savage, uncouth, and thus morally as well as aesthetically contemptible. In Japan, the vernacular terms by which the *Burakumin* have traditionally been designated include both 'four-legged' and 'non-human'. Pejorative stereotyping of people perceived as different is to be found across the whole range of human cultures and societies and it is sustained by evoked, acquired and imposed behaviour-patterns alike: what Byron in his poem *Don Juan* called the 'habit rather blameable' of 'despising those we combat with' serves biological and cultural as well as social functions. But once again, this familiar observation lends additional point to questions about how differences between cultures and societies are to be explained. Why is it that in some the social distance between status-groups is so much larger and the ideological sanctions against social mobility so much more severe than in others? And where they are, what has to happen for the gap to be closed?

One way in which the gap can be closed is by individual mobility on a sufficient scale. Imagine a hypothetical agricultural society in which there is a free market in land but landholding is monopolized by absentee rentiers whose attitude to their tenants is that of the unreconstructed Bolivian *hacendados* to their Indian *colonos*. There doesn't have to be a revolution before the tenants can achieve equality of status with the landowners: if terms of tenure and market conditions are such that land values fall at the same time that tenants can contrive to keep more of their produce for themselves, the tenants may be able to afford to buy out the landowners and the systact of tenants will cease to exist. It's not a very plausible scenario. But there are examples from medieval Europe, Hispanic America, and tsarist Russia where debt-ridden landowners came to be displaced by ambitious tenants (or, it might be, agents or middlemen) whom their grandfathers would have regarded as inferior from birth. And wherever this starts to happen, it's likely to have an exponential effect. In Britain, where women had traditionally been excluded altogether from 'professional' roles, there were still, even as late as the occupational census of 1901, no more than 150 'lady doctors'. But once they were there, and once they were seen to be capable of performing their roles no less competently than their male counterparts, the status of women in general could hardly fail to be raised. It doesn't always work that way. An out-group may suffer discrimination and even persecution all the more because of the resentment aroused by its members' perceived success, as is demonstrated all too clearly by the long history of anti-Semitism around the world. But even in the traditional caste system of Hindu India, a lower-ranked caste could rise in the hierarchy of status if its members all individually adopted the practices of their ritual superiors in a process of what the Indian sociologist M. N. Srinivas calls 'Sanskritization'.[5]

Explanation of mobility, however, still depends on identifying the selective pressures which favour the mutant practices which will bring it about. Under some circumstances, it may be brought about through cultural rather than social changes: attitudes and behaviour towards a hitherto lower-ranked systact are modified by a process of imitation and learning which leads professional athletes, for example, to become role-models even for children of the elite. Or new roles may come into being which are then filled by people who would otherwise fill roles which have ceased to exist: ledger clerks evolve into software programmers and coachmen into motor mechanics. Or mobility may be brought about by direct imposition: governments can intervene to emancipate all slaves, abolish untouchability, give all adults the vote, or remove the restrictions on entry to political or professional roles previously imposed on women, or immigrants, or Roman Catholics, or whoever it may have been; or alternatively, they may dispossess all landowners, exact forced loans from all merchants and businessmen, expel from office all civil servants of 'bad class' bourgeois origins, disenfranchise religious or ethnic minorities, or intern all aliens. But, as in the Bolivian countryside after the 1952 revolution, practices and the roles defined by them have this funny way of reasserting themselves. The Indian government's formal abolition of untouchability didn't stop the 'untouchables' from continuing to be treated as such any more than Mao's attempt to sustain 'permanent revolution' in China did away with the bureaucratic practices and roles which he sought to stigmatize.

The mistake which needs to be avoided is getting the causal relationship the wrong way round. The structure and culture of Indian society isn't a 'caste system' *because* social mobility is virtually nil, but because, through a long distant process still not fully understood, it evolved a rigid hierarchy of endogamous statusgroups performing distinctive functions in the division and specialization of labour. Conversely, a spectacularly high rate of social mobility, either individual or collective, doesn't explain why the society where it occurs is the kind of society it is: the mobility rate is a symptom, not a cause, of what must have been a more

173

or less revolutionary social change. The mobility rate may then have consequences of its own. If, say, all the managers in a post-revolutionary industrial society are replaced by former workers and all their pre-revolutionary powers abolished at a stroke, then, as actually happened in Eastern Europe under Communism, some traditional managerial functions will have to be exercised by agents of the ruling party instead. But the causes and the consequences have both to be studied case by case. The only irrefutable generalizations which can be made are so-called 'impossibility theorems'. You can't give all American citizens a turn at occupying a role in their elected Congress, for the simple reason that the performance of these roles involves a minimum period of incumbency longer than would make it arithmetically possible to do so, and you can't sustain a programme of demoting the 'bad class' elements on the Chinese model for more than one generation, for the simple reason that once the 'bad class' role-incumbents have all been replaced by children of peasants and workers, no others will come to occupy the roles from which, if they could, the programme of permanent revolution would require them to be demoted. But you can't fully understand a society's modes of production, persuasion and coercion without knowing what some sociologists call its 'mobility regime', and whatever its rates of mobility turn out to be they involve by definition a change in the distribution of power among its constituent roles.

Social mobility being as technical a subject as it is, you might think that it is therefore one on which the disjunction between the way in which sociologists analyse it and the subjective experience which the people they write about have of it would be even more acute than on more general topics to do with the structure and culture of the society to which they belong. But it isn't. People who have little or no idea of how the institutions of their society function, or why is has evolved as it has, are likely to be acutely conscious of whether they are rising or falling within it. How much they care is another matter. But nobody moves out of a lower-ranked into a higher-ranked role, or vice versa, without noticing it, or fails to realize that they and those in roles like theirs are being collectively raised or lowered relative to others. Perhaps some British women aged thirty and over were unaware of being enfranchised in 1918, or some French nobles unaware of being stripped of their privileges in 1789. But nobody is unaware of what's happening to them when they are promoted into or dismissed from high office, or when they marry into a much richer or a much poorer family than their own, any more than when they are either incarcerated or released from captivity because they are on the winning or the losing side in a civil war.

So what are social mobility's effects? It was at one time fashionable to argue both that individual upward mobility was a disorienting experience and that those undergoing it were likely to bring with them into their unfamiliar roles the potentially subversive practices and attitudes of their systact of origin. But no convincing evidence has actually been put forward in support of that view. On the contrary, such evidence as there is indicates that upward mobility is a gratifying rather than disorienting experience and that those undergoing it, whether through job change or marriage, cheerfully adopt the practices and attitudes of their systact of destination. I am here talking only of societies like twentieth-century Britain or the United States. In societies like those of the New Guinea Highlands, which have had to evolve within less than two generations from a Stone Age culture into the age of the Internet, the effects of the consequential rates and distances of social mobility may be very different. But in Britain, to go no further, there is no evidence that individual upward mobility is likely to be accompanied by psychological tensions leading to anomic or disruptive behaviour. Nor is there any evidence that those men and women who move out of 'working-class' into 'middle-class' roles bring 'proletarian' attitudes with them: John Goldthorpe, who in the first edition of his book on the results of the Oxford mobility study suggested that they might, quietly deleted the suggestion from the second.

As always, we are dealing with frequencies and probabilities, not universal generalizations. Different people will react to the experience of mobility in different ways, and for the sociologist's (as opposed to the psychologist's) purposes it is the aggregate patterns which need to be explained. But the relation of mobility rates to individual satisfactions and dissatisfactions is, as it happens, the subject of one of the best-known findings in the literature of American sociology: the finding, made during the Second World War, that in a branch of the US army where promotion opportunities were relatively good, satisfaction with promotion opportunities was less than in a branch where they were relatively poor. This finding prompted a particularly influential article by Robert K. Merton and Alice S. Rossi about the theory of 'reference group behaviour' and the concept of 'relative deprivation', as well as a host of subsequent extrapolations and commentaries.[6] But it not only calls for an explanation of the disjunction between objective facts and subjective attitudes; it also invites speculation about the implications for the stability of the institution and the wider society. Although, as I've said, social mobility rates are the consequences rather than the causes of change in the distribution and exercise of economic, ideological and political power, they may come to constitute part of an environment which is more favourable to some mutations of practices than others. It's another of those observations as familiar to the rulers of Ancient Rome as of twentieth-century Britain or the United States that it may be a prudent move to promote the carriers of potentially subversive practices into the elite. Presumably, therefore, there is an optimal mobility rate for the maintenance of a society's existing economic, ideological and political institutions. It's always possible, in social as in natural selection, that some unpredictable external event will have an overriding effect on the society's future evolution from its present modes of production, persuasion and coercion into the next. But the practices defining its constituent roles are more likely to be replicated unchanged if the rate of upward mobility is high enough to siphon off the malcontents but not so high as to generate frustration and resentment among those who will still fail to achieve it.

No sociologist can tell you exactly what 'mobility regime' is in this sense optimal (and it will, of course, be the reverse of 'optimal' to those whose moral and political values lead them to want the current modes of production, persuasion and coercion overturned just as soon as they can be). But the question leads back to the important distinction between individual and collective mobility and the different attitudes which go with them. When the respondents to the Oxford mobility study were asked about their attitudes, it turned out that there was a clear and not unexpected difference between the middle-class and the working-class respondents. People in middle-class occupational roles expect to move up individually over the course of their careers. People in working-class roles look forward instead to collective mobility, if any – that is, to an improvement in their remuneration and conditions of work relative to those above them which is achieved by and on behalf of all the members of their group or category (including, very often, the trade union which helps to bring it about). The difference is readily explicable by reference to their different environments. But it has the further consequence, well-documented in the sociological literature, that working-class parents tend to have very different attitudes to their children's education from middle-class parents. Again, there is nothing irrational in this. What *is* the value to a child who has neither the opportunity nor the motive for a middle-class career of what a working-class boy interviewed in the 1960s called 'maths, history – all that crap'? But then what about the substantial minority of working-class children who *are* going to have middle-class careers? The British studies in which they too are interviewed contain much descriptive evidence of the tensions within families and peer-groups to which this can give rise. For example: 'when I got to Ash Grange and wore the uniform, the other children used to shout about that. I didn't mind so much. I felt superior. But I had a violin as well, and I used to dread carrying that violin case ... that brought me more bashings than anything else.'[7] Experiences like that one are, like the rates of mobility bound up with them, symptoms rather than causes of social change. But they're all too vivid for the children whose experiences they are, and they're a long way from the impersonal calculations which place these children in the bottom left-hand cell of the table on page 162.

The converse, however, is the experience of the people in the top right-hand cell. The British sociologists who have interviewed the downwardly mobile have found that the experience was, as the authors of one study put it, 'usually unacknowledged and psychologically quite unacceptable';[8] or as Goldthorpe puts it, 'with the exception of one or two who had suffered the collapse of their own businesses, our downwardly mobile men were reluctant to recognize themselves as being failures in any total or decisive way'.[9] At this point, we touch on one of those aspects of subjective experience on which the fullest and most authentic descriptive evidence is more likely to come from novels, autobiographies and memoirs than from interviews conducted by sociologists on the doorsteps of the households which have fallen into their samples. To give a characteristically uncharitable example by the playwright John Osborne in his description of his mother's and father's families, 'Coming Down in the World was something the Groves had in common with the Osbornes, except that the Groves had come to feel less sense of grievance, looking on it as the justified price of profligate living or getting above yourself, rather than as a cruel trick of destiny or a creeping army of upstarts Getting the Better of their Betters.'[10] You may say, and rightly so, that what the Osbornes and Groves think about it tells us nothing of any significance about the workings and evolution of British society or about the determinants of the rates of either upward or downward mobility within it. But the point of the quotation is to bring out just how keenly felt are the experiences which underlie the numbers in the mobility table – much more so than the figures in the Registrar-General's decennial census reports, or the data from the General Household Survey on the distribution of incomes, or the political scientists' cross-tabulations of voting behaviour by 'social class'.

There is still a disjunction. But it's a disjunction between what is (statistically) and what feels like (subjectively) the importance of chance in determining who goes up and who goes down. Ernest Bevin, the untutored carter from the Bristol dockside who rose to be Minister of Labour under Churchill and Foreign Secretary under Attlee, was right both statistically and subjectively when he described himself as 'a turn-up in a million'.[11] But for many other British people, what feels like luck is really the arithmetic of the mobility tables and what feels like the reward of effort is really luck. The autobiographies of the mobile often reflect a mixture of gratification and surprise at the sequence of coincidences which has brought them from their point of origin to their point of destination in social space; but their authors might have been less surprised, and perhaps also less gratified, if they could have realized at the time how many vacant roles would have to be filled by incumbents from origins like theirs. Conversely, those autobiographies which reflect a sense of well-merited achievement often fail to register a sense of the degree to which, once the vacancies are there, the process by which one person rather than another rises to occupy them may not, after all, be as 'meritocratic' as it suits the successful candidates to believe. On the topic of social

IX

Possible and Impossible Worlds

SUPPOSE THAT ONE FINE DAY you're passing a building-site in London or New York where the hard-hatted construction workers are taking a break, and you pause within earshot to listen to their conversation. To your surprise, it turns out to be about twentieth-century poetry. One of them is arguing for Ezra Pound's *Cantos*, another for Wallace Stevens, and a third for John Berryman, while a fourth is insistent that only Eliot, Yeats and early (but not late) Auden deserve to be elevated to the pantheon of twentieth-century Anglo-American literature. Impossible? It's not as if an anthropologist were to come back from the Kalahari Desert claiming to have found a pristine !Kung San band who have evolved a domestic electronics industry from within their foraging economy, or a biologist were to claim to have discovered that elephants did, after all, precede bacteria. Even if the hard-hats on the building site are *real* construction workers, not students doing vacation jobs or actors rehearsing a movie, who says a construction worker can't have a genuine taste for, and informed interest in, twentieth-century poetry? I remember an evening I spent as a graduate student in California with two veteran members of the West Coast Longshoremen's Union called 'Mitch' and 'Blackie'; it was Mitch, as I recall, who was an enthusiastic collector of first editions of nineteenth-century poetry, particularly Wordsworth. But all the same, do you seriously believe that the scene on the building-site which I've just invented has ever happened? And if not, why not?

Contrast that example with this one. You are the foreign observer invited to witness the success of the new revolutionary regime in a Third World country in ridding itself of neo-colonialist influences and putting political power into the hands of the indigenous people. The new regime has allegedly dismantled the undemocratic authority structure inherited from the colonial period and replaced it with a system of workers' soviets and village communes in which all decisions are taken by majority vote and carried out by elected representatives. All surplus resources flowing from the farms and factories are used to finance free social services, including housing, health and education. The ruling political party takes no major decisions of policy without submitting them to a referendum in which all adult citizens take part. There is no intellectual or artistic censorship, no intrusion by the agents of the state into domestic life, no conscription of labour, no inequality of wages or salaries, no restriction on movement from place to place, no unemployment, and no crime. The lessons of past revolutions (you are assured) have been learnt, and the ideals of liberty, equality and fraternity fulfilled at last. Do you believe it – *all* of it, that is? And again: if not, why not?

Some states of the world are *logically* impossible, and where that's so there's nothing more to be said. But it isn't always as easy to tell as you might suppose. It came as a big surprise to a lot of people when in 1951 the consequently Nobel prizewinning American economist Kenneth. J. Arrow, in a monograph entitled *Social Choice and Individual Values*, that proved our intuitive criteria for 'democratic' decision-making – that is, decisions arrived at by adding up the preferences of everyone involved – can't be satisfied unless we're prepared to accept under certain conditions an ordering of those preferences which is either 'imposed' or 'dictatorial'. Similarly, many of the writers in the long tradition of anarchist political theory never grasped the inescapability of the conclusion that if, as they argued, inequality and violence in human societies are due to the perversion of innate human goodness by the wicked institution of government, the wicked institution of government must have been impossible in the first place since innately good human beings could never have created it. By contrast, it is – for the time being, at least – an empirical fact that you can't have a society in which every child born lives to be 100 years old. But it's often surprisingly difficult, when trying to establish whether a hypothetical state of the world is impossible or not, to be sure just what kind of impossibility it is, if it is. In a 'feudal' society, a man who had freely commended himself to another man as his 'liege lord' couldn't, by definition, swear allegiance to another without repudiating the first. Couldn't? On the contrary, they did it all the time. The effective constraint, such as it was, on their behaviour wasn't that they couldn't *say* to two different people, 'I tie myself exclusively to you, my lord', but that if the two different lords to whom they had said so went to war with each other, not even the craftiest vassal could fight on both sides at once. But again: couldn't? It's neither logically nor empirically impossible to change sides at half-time.

Let's go back for a moment to social mobility. In Chapter VIII, I gave two examples of impossibilities: not every middle-class role can be filled by a child of middle-class parents, and not every child of working-class parents can join the elite. But what about a regime of 'perfect mobility' as expounded in the first large-scale study of social mobility carried out in Britain, that by Professor David Glass and associates which was published in 1954?[1] 'Perfect' mobility, for Glass, would be a state of society in which the association between fathers' and sons' occupations was statistically random: male children would be no more or less likely to occupy the same category of occupational role as their fathers than any other. From this starting-point the figures in any actual mobility table can be contrasted, as Glass in fact does, with the 'perfect' figures and the appropriate inferences about inequality of opportunity in British society drawn. You may well think that it's an odd use of the term 'perfection', and suspect that Glass was not only a talented demographer (which he was) but also a left-wing AM who wanted to persuade his readers that rates of individual upward mobility in British society were lower than they ought to be. 'Perfect' mobility may be neither logically nor empirically *impossible*. But even if it isn't, it might as well be. This is partly because of the statistical improbability of the 'perfect' numbers in the cells of a 7×7 mobility table ever being matched by the actuals: nothing in the real world ever works out as neatly as that. But it's also because of the sociological and psychological reasons for which, in all sorts of societies including twentieth-century Britain and the United States, sons are quite often inclined to follow in their fathers' footsteps, whether as farmers, actors, businessmen or thieves.

But now consider the following proposition which was put forward by Sidney and Beatrice Webb in their book *Industrial Democracy*, of which a second edition was published just after the First World War. They were addressing, in their indefatigably earnest way, the evolution of 'collective bargaining' – a term which had been coined in 1891 by Beatrice herself – between employers and unionized employees, and in 1919 they looked forward to a well-ordered state of the world in which union officials would, as they put it, perform like lawyers a function which 'could, with equal propriety, be rendered to either client'.[2] It would be hard to argue that such a thing is totally impossible. There have, after all, been trade union officials who have seen it as their function to reach compromises which they believe to be in the best interests of both labour and management and to avoid confrontations of the kind which they believe can only do damage to both sets of interests. But all the same, how can the elected representatives of one party to a negotiation properly render the *same* service to the *other* party? Union officials might possibly agree that bargaining with employers should be conducted not by themselves but by professional negotiators, and the professional negotiators might be people who *were* like lawyers in that they offered their services, at least in theory, to either side. But the function of the unions themselves, and therefore of their own officials, could only cease to be adversarial in a world in which there was nothing to bargain collectively about. The example doesn't explain why British industrial relations have evolved as they have. But it does help to explain why the critics of the Webbs from the Right and the Left alike have so often accused them of naivety.

But now we are starting to tread on more treacherous ground. It may be easy to cull from the writings of sociologists predictions and proposals whose naivety is glaringly obvious in hindsight. But it's equally easy to point to predictions and proposals which were dismissed as naive at the time when they were made but turned out to be nothing of the sort. Some of Marx's and Engels's *Communist Manifesto* itself is in that category, starting with their anticipation of progressive income tax and free schooling for all children. Just as some of the physicists who might have been supposed to be best qualified to judge turned out to be wrong about the possibility of nuclear weapons, so have some of the best-informed commentators on social and political affairs turned out to be wrong about the possibility of hitherto unthought-of institutional arrangements and the constituent roles and their defining practices which would sustain them. 'Universal adult suffrage, Mr Bentham? In early nineteenth-century Britain? Come, come, my good Sir, you speak in jest.' If one of Aristotle's pupils had told him that it would be perfectly possible to envisage a world without slavery, the young man would probably have been given as short shrift as a young officer who said to Clausewitz in 1813, after he returned from fighting against Napoleon in Russia to fight against him in his native Prussia, that it would be perfectly possible to envisage a world without war. And what would Goethe, the world-famous exemplar of German culture, have said if asked to envisage a world in which a ruler of mid-twentieth-century Germany who had, at the crucial point of his political career, been democratically elected would then proceed to organize first the ostracism, then the persecution, and finally the extermination of the Jewish population, both in Germany and in the territories which Germany had by then proceeded to occupy by force of arms?

Part of the difficulty is Popper's: you can't know what future generations are going to know until they know it. There was no way that Aristotle could even formulate the proposition that it might be naive to refuse to believe in the possibility of nuclear weapons, genetic engineering and public opinion polls. But it's also that the sceptics, who can be so good at presenting themselves as worldly-wise, hard-nosed street-smarts, sometimes turn out to be more naive than the innocent and credulous. Anybody in the year 1600 who said that the rise and fall of the tide was to be explained by the moon was no more likely to be believed than Herodotus to believe that the Neurians were once-a-year werewolves. But then along comes Isaac Newton with the concept of gravity, and the rest, as they say, is history.

Utopian sociology has a history of its own which goes back long before Sir Thomas More in 1516 published the book which gave 'utopia' the meaning we now attach to it. Much of it is hardly less fanciful than the Isles of the Blessed, Shangri-la, or the Big Rock Candy Mountain. But dedicated social alchemists from Plato to B. F. Skinner, whose *Walden Two* describes a Behaviorist Utopia of supposedly benevolent 'operant conditioning' which would send any normal social animal screaming into orbit,[3] have convinced themselves that they have discovered a way to make human beings conform to their ideal of the Good Society. How good it would really be, even if it could really exist, is for you to decide in accordance with your own moral and political values. But sociologists have to take such ideas seriously, not simply because their proponents themselves do but because there are people who have been prepared to devote their lives to making them come true. However laughable we may think the ideas of the nineteenth-century French utopian socialist Charles Fourier, one of whose more eccentric proposals was that since small boys like playing with dirt they should be given the job of garbage disposal, Fourierist communities based on what would nowadays be called 'communitarian' ideals were actually established after his death in the United States, and they didn't all collapse in chaos and strife immediately, any more than the monastic orders of the European Middle Ages all collapsed immediately into laxity and corruption. However many alchemical social experiments end in ridicule and tears, nobody can be absolutely certain that the same will happen with the next one, or the one after next. I'm only in a position to call them alchemical because even their most passionate sympathizers have no choice but to recognize that they *have* failed. But nobody can say for certain what works and what doesn't until somebody gives it a try.

It is, accordingly, more rewarding to consider what is and isn't possible by looking to see what lessons can be drawn from societies which have shown what's improbably possible by doing it. The danger is that people will be too ready to see what they want to see: Sidney and Beatrice Webb were, along with many others in the 1930s, even more naive about the Soviet Union than Margaret Mead in the 1920s about Samoa. Here is Petrarch in the year 1364 writing about Venice: 'the one hope today of liberty, peace, and justice, the one refuge of honourable men . . . rich in fame, mighty in her resources but mightier in virtue, solidly built on marble but standing more solid on a foundation of civic concord, ringed with salt waters but more secure with the salt of good counsel.'[4] A utopian view, all right. But Venice *was* remarkable in the stability and prosperity which it achieved through a unique set of practices and roles including its doge, its interlocking councils and overlapping ballots, its mercantile bourgeoisie, its seamen and craftsmen, its patriotic cult of St Mark, and not least its secret police. The anonymous observer of its institutions as they were in the mid-eleventh century who annotated a contemporary document with the surprised remark (in Latin) that 'that people neither ploughs nor sows nor grows vines' would no doubt have been even more surprised to see how well that people had managed to do for themselves by the time of Petrarch's encomium. But the reasons for which contemporary observers found Venice so surprising are also reasons for saying that there must be a lesson about possible worlds to be learned from it. It's not a question of whether it was the model of liberty, peace and justice which Petrarch proclaims it to be. Of course it wasn't. For a start, the murder of Doge Vitale II Michiel in the doorway of San Zaccaria in AD 1172 is strikingly reminiscent of the murder of Tiberius Gracchus in the Forum at Rome in 133 BC, and Republican Rome was a society where, as we have seen, liberty, peace and justice were in notably short supply. What Venice shows is that a quite unprecedented set of economic, ideological and political institutions can be created and maintained from quite exceptionally inauspicious beginnings.

It's accordingly a perfectly sensible sociological exercise to indulge in a little of what might be called realistic utopianism. A good recent example is a short book by Alec Nove, lately professor of economics at Glasgow University, under the title *The Economics of Feasible Socialism*, which was published six years before the Soviet Union's collapse in 1989. It may seem an odd choice, since the topic is one which, no less than slavery in the ancient world, is bedevilled by Finley's 'dogma, pseudo-issues, and moral judgements'. But like the mere existence of Venice, the mere existence of the Soviet Union between 1917 and 1989 raises some pertinent questions about what's sociologically possible and what isn't. Nove is well aware of the irony that Marx, whose ideas were at least notionally the inspiration for the Russian Revolution, was as ready to denounce utopianism in others as he was to indulge in it himself.

But Nove is consistently cautious in the manner in which he addresses the question whether a set of institutions still recognizably 'socialist' could avoid what he sees (and deplores) as the 'deformations' of the socialist ideal: self-serving bureaucracy, wasteful allocation of resources, centralization of coercive power, undemocratic decision-making, and so forth. He is quite clear that the so-called 'withering away of the state' is a fantasy, that there has to be a distinction between the roles of governors and governed, and that contracts have to be legally enforceable. But he cannot see why, for example, the boundary between the public and market sectors of an industrial economy shouldn't be decided by democratic vote, or large-scale private ownership of the means of production abolished, or income differentials determined centrally rather than by the market, or workers given the option of work in co-operatives or own-account businesses as alternatives to enterprises owned by the state.

No sociologist can plausibly claim to have a definitive answer to the question of how plausible or not institutional arrangements of this kind might be. But speculative sociology like this serves, if nothing else, to clarify the important distinction between the improbably possible (Venice) and the probably impossible (democratic socialism as Nove would like to see it). Many commentators on the Russian Revolution have remarked on the irony that the groups who most welcomed it, notably the peasantry, then suffered most from it and that it was sustained only by recourse to the means of coercion in the hands of the state on a scale and to a degree far beyond what had been practised under the supposed autocracy of the tsars: the British historian Orlando Figes's widely praised account of it, published in 1997, is aptly titled *A People's Tragedy*. But if to some the conclusion which follows is that the constraints on possible worlds imposed by natural, cultural and social selection alike make nonsense of everything that Marx so confidently predicted and desired, to others the conclusion is that next time a wiser as well as a kinder Lenin will know how a genuinely democratic socialism can, after all, be achieved.

You will not, however, be surprised when I say that the conclusion *I* want to draw is the need for these arguments to be conducted within the terms expounded in this book. 'Success', in sociology as opposed to moral and political philosophy, is no more (or less) than the environmental conditions which permit a set of mutant practices and the roles defined by them to be replicated and diffused in such a way as to sustain a distinctive set of economic, ideological, and political institutions over successive generations. If and when a Nove-like set of mutations actually happens, the hope must be that there are some good sociologists around to study it: just think how much more we might now understand about the distribution and exercise of power in general, and the causes of, say, the Fall of the Roman Republic or the French Revolution in particular, if Max Weber had been there at the time with access to all the relevant evidence: he in fact lived long enough to see the Russian Revolution, and his sceptical reaction to it was amply vindicated after his death. There is certainly no harm in speculating about the probably impossible. But the improbably possible is what social evolution is all about.

Behind all this, however, lurks the issue of what the philosophers call 'counterfactual conditionals'. Any proffered explanation of any sequence or process of cultural and social, as of biological, evolution implies the truth of a proposition about what would have happened otherwise. If the asteroid hadn't struck, the dinosaurs wouldn't have been wiped out. The Roman Republic wouldn't have fallen, or at any rate not then, if the Senate had redistributed the land and reformed the rules governing the tenure of political roles. To the congenital sceptics, assertions like these are a good reason for telling sociologists, among others, that they can't really explain anything, since you can never know for sure the truth of a proposition which by your own admission is about a world that never existed. But the congenital sceptics don't in practice need to be taken any more seriously than the congenital relativists. So what, if I can't *prove* to you that if I hadn't stepped on the banana skin I wouldn't have fallen flat on my face?

On the other hand, the sceptics are quite right to be dismissive of the kind of speculative sociology which dabbles in 'what if?' questions of a wholly unanswerable kind. Pascal famously raised the question whether history would have been different if Cleopatra's nose had been so shaped that she wasn't, after all, sexually irresistible to visiting Roman generals, and there was at one time quite a fashion for academic exercises on what would (supposedly) have happened if Napoleon had won the Battle of Waterloo or the Persians the Battle of Marathon. Such questions do have their uses in sociology as elsewhere in science. But the useful ones have to be distinguished from the useless. There's no simple rule by which to do so. It's not a question of what kind of institution or society you're studying, or in what part of the world, or how long ago. 'What if Napoleon had won at Waterloo?' is a useless question, since there's no possible way of knowing whether it would have made a big difference or, because the Allies would have defeated him thereafter anyway, none at all to the subsequent history of Europe. But 'what if no Protestant Reformation in Europe?' has, thanks largely to Weber, turned out to be a useful one, since it has led to a great deal of detailed and illuminating research into the importance or otherwise of religious ideology in economic development. I've accordingly chosen two examples of what seem to me to be useful counterfactual speculations, a large-scale one from the very beginning of social evolution and a small-scale one from a problem in applied sociology in my own society in my own lifetime.

The first one has the additional merit of showing how a genuinely 'Darwinian' sociology, far from lending support to the doctrines of 'Social Darwinism', actually shows how badly the Social Darwinists got it wrong. It's a familiar observation about the history of mankind that 'our' (i.e. Christian European) culture was carried by people from 'our' societies into Asia, Africa, the Americas and Australia rather than the other way round. Although Macaulay in 1840 asked his readers to picture a New Zealander one day contemplating the ruins of St Paul's,[5] it's not as if 'their' explorers, missionaries, traders, settlers, colonists and conquistadors in fact imposed their practices, doctrines and technologies on 'us' rather than the other way round. But what would have had to happen, or be the case, for them to do so?

The Social Darwinists' answer was that they wouldn't and couldn't because Europeans were the superior race in terms of intellectual and cognitive capacity. But we now know that can't be right, because there simply hasn't been a long enough time or sufficient selective pressure for the descendants of the human beings who after the initial dispersion out of Africa settled in Europe to be differentiated, genetically speaking, from those who settled elsewhere. It's long enough to have given Europeans paler faces and Australians darker ones because of the consistent difference in climate. But it hasn't given Europeans different minds; and minds are what it's all about. In the words of the Italian geneticist Luca Cavalli-Sforza, it's because the changes in body surface required by climatic differences are externally visible that they strike us so forcibly, 'and we automatically assume that differences of similar magnitude exist below the surface, in the rest of our genetic material. This is simply not so: the remainder of our genetic makeup hardly differs at all.'[6] It's true that we are, as always, dealing in probabilities and that initially small variations between populations can widen progressively over time. But it's overwhelmingly improbable that between-group variations in inborn cognitive capacity could have become significantly greater than within-group variations over the period in question. If, 50,000 years ago, God had picked up every human being in Europe and deposited them all in Australia, and had at the same time deposited the ancestors of the present day Australian 'aborigines' in Europe, then the Europeans would have evolved a culture similar to the aboriginal Australian and the Australians a culture similar to the European. The same environment would have imposed the same selective pressures on the different members of the same subspecies, and by the time that explorers from eighteenth-century Europe made contact with the Australian continent they would have found societies as elaborately organized and ingeniously adapted to Australian conditions as was in fact the case. You may say that nobody can *prove* this, and that there might still have been sufficient differences between and within the two populations for the course of cultural and social evolution to have taken a number of different turns about which it would indeed be fruitless to speculate. But that doesn't undermine the conclusion which *can* be drawn from the counterfactual hypothesis: the racist answer to the original question is overwhelmingly implausible.

My second speculation concerns the creation of a so-called 'welfare state' in Britain after the Second World War. The conventional view is that it was the result of the war and the victory of the Labour Party in the General Election of 1945 – the counterfactual implication being that if the Conservatives had won, there would never have been the same degree of collective provision by the state. Although the Conservatives, when returned to power in 1951, made no attempt to dismantle it, this was, according to the conventional wisdom, only because they were well aware that it would lose them a great many votes if they did. Churchill's dislike of William Beveridge, whose Report of 1944 was the cardinal document of post-war welfare policy, was well known, and· the 1945 election, in which Churchill imprudently threatened the electorate with the bogey of a Socialist 'Gestapo' in the event of a Labour victory, was as intensely fought as any that followed it. The welfare legislation passed by the Labour government was thus the culmination of a long history of left-wing reformism which the egalitarian sense of common hardship generated by the war, coupled with the resentment directed at those seen as responsible for the miseries and failures of the inter-war years, had at long last brought to fruition.

There are, however, two things wrong with this story. The first is that by 1944 there was already widespread agreement on the need for some form of national health service and for the further extension of unemployment benefits beyond what had been available before the war. The second is that the assumptions on which the post-war legislation was based were highly unrealistic, and its Conservative opponents were to that extent vindicated. A world in which unlimited medical care could indefinitely be delivered free of charge on demand was even more probably impossible than one in which, as Beveridge envisaged, the working population would always consist overwhelmingly of male breadwinners heading households with wives and children, and single mothers would almost all be widows or divorcees. And as we saw in Chapter VII, the hated practice of means-testing, which Labour politicians of the '40s believed to have been abolished once and for all, was so far from being so that in 1990 more than one British household in three had at least one member who was at least partly dependent on a means-tested benefit. So although I can't of course *prove* it, it's plausible to suppose that even if Churchill had won the 1945 election, Britain's system of social welfare half a century later would have been much the same as it in fact evolved into being.

Although, in Chapter VII, I reacted with outspoken dismay to the idea that sociologists would make better politicians than politicians, there might appear still to be room for the idea that politicians should use sociologists as guides, philosophers and friends. Beveridge's career is, however, a persuasive argument to the contrary. This isn't said in criticism of his abilities. But he was constantly changing his mind, he was apt to be both obstinate and defensive about his ideas, and to the extent that his injunctions to policy-makers rested on his predictions of the future he was almost always wrong. Indeed, it's because his Report became, contrary to his own or Churchill's or anybody else's original expectations, so famous a document that it points so clearly to the conclusion encapsulated in Joel Cohen's 'Law of Prediction'. Nobody disputes that politicians can benefit from informed advice, whether it comes from colleagues, officials, academics, journalists, or anybody else. But it needs to be advice, not prophecy. Prophecy is always readily available for rulers who want it. But its value is no different today from what it was when the kings of Persia were consulting the Magi whom Herodotus describes.

X

Uses and Abuses

USES? ABUSES? Isn't the question whether a body of knowledge is well or badly applied one for moral philosophers to argue about?

Indeed so. It's a question of morals, not of physics, whether President Truman was right to order the dropping of atomic bombs on Hiroshima and Nagasaki in 1945. It's a question of morals, not of biology, whether parents ought to be allowed the option of genetically re-engineering their unborn children. It's a question of morals, not of sociology, whether democratically elected governments should be entitled to prolong their tenure of office by deliberate manipulation of the media. But there's an obvious difference. You can't have a physics of physics, or a biology of biology. But you can't avoid having a sociology of sociology, since sociology is itself one of those human social activities of which sociology is the study. Add to that the equally obvious fact that human beings all have their own moral and political views about the kind of groups, communities, institutions and societies that they would most like to belong to in their various roles, and you have a problem which no natural scientist ever has to face.

Once again, there's an enormous academic literature on this, much of it written by people who don't agree at all that sociology and substitute religion belong in separate university departments and on separate library shelves. If you think they're right, I doubt whether anything in this chapter is going to persuade you otherwise. But you will, even so, be bound to acknowledge that the sociology of sociology raises issues of different kinds which need to be distinguished from one another as clearly as they can.

The first is the issue of relativism, which (some will say) I dismissed too hastily when it came up in Chapter II. Although (they will concede) no enquiry about anything in the world can be meaningfully conducted without *a* notion of truth and falsehood – as Clemenceau once said, nobody is ever going to claim that the First World War was started by the Belgian army's invasion of Germany – it doesn't follow that sociological knowledge is necessarily privileged over other ways of looking at the world. Isn't the lesson of the sociology of sociology (they will ask) that sociology is just another internally coherent but fundamentally arbitrary myth?

To answer that question, it isn't enough just to say, true though it is, that the people who ask it lead their own lives *as if* sociological knowledge was for real. That, after all, is no different from Evans-Pritchard adapting to life among the Azande by behaving as if he too believed in witches. The better answer is simply to reaffirm that science is defined as such by its own criterion of public testability. The relativists are likely to reply that the criterion of public testability is itself part of the self-serving myth. But then there are myths and myths, and myths that can be put to the test by any observer who chooses to do so are a different kind of myth from those that can't. What sociologist wouldn't like to have myths to draw on as successful as those on which molecular biologists can draw? Besides, the relativists are going to have to admit, when pressed, that they don't and can't have a criterion of their own by which the criterion of public testability can be overturned, since if nothing can truly be found out then nor can the proposition that nothing can truly be found out. This knock-down point was well made as long ago as Plato's *Euthydemus*: if the idea of getting anything right or wrong is meaningless, then how can the person who wants to teach us so claim to have anything to teach?

That, however, is a quite different kind of sociology of sociology from the kind concerned to explain why sociologists believe what they do believe, what social and psychological influences lie behind the research by which they have been led to those beliefs, and the reasons for which the results of their researches are or aren't believed by their colleagues and the wider public. Questions of this kind lead to mystery stories no less fascinating than any other kind of sociological investigation. To go no further, look at the sociology of Marxism and its quite extraordinary influence both on academic research and on political movements from China to Peru. But they are questions to be addressed in the same way whatever branch of intellectual enquiry is being, so to say, sociologized. Geology is in this respect no different from sociology. I have already remarked that the views of nineteenth-century geologists were influenced by their views about the Bible, and the story of the controversies which divided them and the sequence of events by which these controversies came to be resolved is revealing not only about their individual prejudices and obstinacies but about the organization of science in Victorian England and its relation to the structure and culture of British society as a whole. And when it comes to the twentieth century, there is a curiously similar story to be told about the initial reluctance of many geologists to accept the 'geoscience revolution' which introduced to a hostile establishment the now orthodox notions of tectonic plates and continental drift.[1] But this has nothing to do with questions about the justification for what comes to be recognized to be true. People do sometimes deliberately confuse the two, as when German Fascists refused to accept the results of 'Jewish' physics and Russian Communists the findings of 'bourgeois' biology. But anyone who seriously thinks that the origin of a belief has any logical bearing on its validity needs only to be reminded of Descola's choice, as I described it in Chapter VI, between taking his companion to be cured of salpingitis by the local Amazonian shaman and taking her to be cured by 'Western' antibiotics at the nearest mission station.

But there is a third kind of sociology of sociology, which for the purpose of this concluding chapter is the most important one. Having asked 'are sociologists entitled to be sure that what they're saying is correct?' and 'what has led them to say it in the belief that it *is* correct?', you are still faced with the question 'but what are they doing in saying it?' Take for example the following passage from the British sociologists John Westergaard and Henrietta Resler:

The share of all personal wealth owned by just the richest 1 per cent of the adult population was probably near 30 per cent around 1970. This rough figure excludes the value of formal entitlements to pensions: reasonably so, in our view, since even the benefits of private occupational pension schemes are uncertain – as we have pointed out earlier – while state pensions are determined by changing public policy and involve no rights that can be sold or passed on to others. The estimate, too, makes some allowance for understatement of the value of income-yielding property in the data available – hardly full allowance, when it is remembered that well over a third of all income from property reported for tax in 1971 was in the hands of a 1 per cent minority. Ownership of small property which yields no taxable income – owner-occupied housing, motor cars, household goods and personal effects, for example – is spread much more widely of course, though still unevenly; and the limit in value below which these things can hardly rate as 'property' is debatable. But whatever the precise share of the 1 per cent minority – above or below some 30 per cent – it is very large. And with 5 per cent of the adult population holding something like half the total in their hands, the concentration is enormous. Except in so far as many now own – or are buying – the homes they live in, considerable sections of the salaried groups, as well as the mass of wage earners, are excluded from property ownership of any substance.[2]

This may look, at first sight, like an extract from a boring article in an academic journal of economics or (more boring still) statistics in which the authors are struggling with the problems of definition and measurement associated with plotting a frequency distribution of the kind illustrated in Chapter IV. But you don't need to look at it for long before you realize that it's something more than that. The authors are attitude-peddling for all they're worth. Their not very hidden agenda is to persuade their readers that capitalism is wicked and the distribution of wealth in contemporary Britain a Bad Thing.

The Oxford philosopher J. L. Austin made what is in this context the critical point when he analysed the distinction between the three different 'speech-acts' which he called 'locution', 'illocution' and 'perlocution'.[3] Locution is the act of asserting, as Westergaard and Resler do, that 1% of the population own 30% of the wealth. Illocution is what they are doing *in* asserting it – implying what a bad thing it is. Perlocution is what they seek to achieve *by* asserting it – rousing their readers to a state of righteous indignation. The distinction is by no means unproblematic, as Austin himself was well aware. But it can be extremely useful to readers of sociological texts uncertain about how they are, in the currently fashionable term, to 'deconstruct' them. What exactly is the conclusion of which the author is seeking to persuade them? The illocutionary function, in Austin's terminology, of any sociological text is likely to be a good deal more than simply reporting a set of sociological facts which the author believes to be true. At the very least, it is likely to imply some sort of explanation of the observations which the author has chosen to report, even if it doesn't extend also to the attempt to describe to the reader what it felt like to be one of the people whose social behaviour the report is about. But it may be any number of other things in addition or instead. The author may, for example, turn out to be proposing to the reader a taxonomy of institutions and societies of the kind I have admitted that we badly need, or extrapolating (however misguidedly) from the present state of the society chosen for study a vision of its long-term future, or undermining the credibility of some rival sociologist, or demonstrating to the reader the value of a chosen methodology, or (as Descola's *Spears of Twilight* does, among other things) taking the reader through the process of enquiry by which the sociologist was led to the conclusions to which the reader's assent is being sought. However straightforward the answer may turn out to be, the question 'what is the author doing in saying all this?' is always worth asking.

Notice, however, that whatever answer the reader may be disposed to give, and whether or not the author may be disposed to accept it, there is no more comfort to be drawn therefrom by the sceptics than by the relativists. They are quite entitled to argue, as they will, that sociologists who think that in saying what they say they are reporting to their readers facts about human social behaviour, or explaining to their readers why those facts are as they are, are deluding themselves. But the only way to persuade *us* that we are deluding ourselves will be to show us that our observations are contradicted by those of other observers and our explanations invalidated by the greater success of alternative hypotheses in accounting for the same set of observations. No doubt it is often the case that we do delude ourselves: we see what we want to see, we dismiss too quickly the ideas of other sociologists, we trust our own explanations too readily, and we don't take hostile criticism as seriously as we should. Moreover, we are bound to accept that even our most convincing-looking results may be overtaken by our successors. But to admit all this is at the same time to reaffirm our conviction that some observations can indeed be shown to the satisfaction of all observers to be more accurate than others and some explanations to stand up better than others against any proposed alternatives. To attack us because we aren't as good as we think we are at what we think we're doing is very different from denying that we're doing what we think we're doing at all.

Nor am I, in appealing to Austin's distinction, conceding any-thing to those who seek to maintain that sociology is a philosophi-cal rather than a scientific activity. Sociologists can, and often do, make mistakes which are mistakes of a philosophical rather than a scientific kind, like Durkheim's claim that our conception of duality is to be explained by dualities being 'social facts' in his question-begging sense of that term. But that's not an argument for saying that they're doing philosophy rather than science. It's only to say that sociologists can benefit, as we undoubtedly can, from the help of philosophers under Bertrand Russell's definition of what philosophers do. Philosophy, said Russell, is the discipline which teaches you how to tell a good argument from a bad one; and in the literature of sociology there are plenty of both.

What, then, is the help that Austin's distinction can give in the analysis of what is to be counted as 'abuse'?

It hardly needs saying that sociologists oughtn't to buy their PhD theses on the black market, deliberately falsify their research findings, or publish other people's ideas as their own – 'oughtn't', that is, by the standards of academic integrity. If you're the head of the German Census Bureau in the year that Hitler launches the Final Solution, you may well feel an overriding moral duty *not* to hand over to the Gestapo the correct addresses at which men and women of Jewish birth are to be found. But there are subtler forms of what is meant by intellectual 'bad faith' or, in the famous title of a book which hardly anybody who cites it (including myself) has actually read, the *'trahison des clercs'*.[4]

Like many other forms of misbehaviour, bad faith is easier to detect than to define. But its essence consists in passing off one illocutionary act for another. With the example which I quoted from Westergaard and Resler, no reader can be in serious doubt about what's going on. But there are all sorts of other ways in which the results of sociological enquiry can be so presented that the reader is led to think that the author is doing something other than what he or she actually *is* doing. Indeed, it is this which gives the critics of sociology, whether on the Left or on the Right, grounds for their often justified suspicions that proclamations of objectivity and disinterestedness are not to be taken at face value. The observations may be demonstrably accurate, the techniques used to analyse them impeccable, the hypotheses advanced to explain them as rigorously tested as they can be. But why *these* observations, *these* techniques, and *these* hypotheses? Time and again, whether the topic is the performance in American schools and universities of students of African-American descent, or the changes in the proportion of the British labour force who belong to trade unions, or the failure of land reform in pre-Revolutionary Russia, or the rates of inter-generational mobility from the bourgeoisie into the nobility in *ancien régime* France, or a comparison between peasant uprisings in seventeenth-century Europe and seventeenth-century China, or even the transition from slavery to dependent tenancy in the Late Roman Empire or the relative significance of Gallic and Teutonic institutions in the evolution of 'feudalism', readers who suspect that their assent is being solicited to something more than is explicitly set out on the printed page will be vindicated. 'Bad faith', in this context, is simply failure to be candid with the reader about what it is.

Max Weber, who was as aware as anybody of the issue, sought to resolve it by distinguishing between 'value-neutrality' (the idea, as I put it in Chapter I, that nobody can seriously dispute that the validity of an explanation of why the state of the world is what it is is logically independent of value-judgements about whether that state of the world is good or bad) and 'value-relevance' (the idea that the choice of what to explain is a function of the interests and values of the researcher whose choice it is). Stated in these terms, it is a legitimate and useful distinction. The trouble, however, is that Weber was concerned to use it as the answer to a different question – the question, much debated among Weber's contemporaries, of what differentiates the sciences of human behaviour from the sciences of nature. To *that* question, the answer is the same as to the question whether science in general can be distinguished from myth: 'value-relevance' is just as relevant to the sciences of nature, whose objects of study are inanimate, as to the sciences whose subject-matter raises issues of moral and political philosophy. One simple illustration will (I hope) be enough. A factual statement, like Westergaard and Resler's about the distribution of wealth in Britain, may have, and be intended to have, the perlocutionary effect of encouraging its readers to oppose the political party whose administration has allowed the reported distribution to come about. But so, equally, may a factual statement about the chemical properties of Semtex have and be intended to have the perlocutionary effect of encouraging its readers into the streets to try and blow up the nearest police station. In either case, the issue of bad faith comes back to Austin's distinction and the question whether the author is being honest with the reader about what the author is doing in, and perhaps therefore by, asserting facts and proffering explanations which are value-neutral in themselves.

Full-blooded *trahison des clercs* is something else again, if you take it to mean not merely bad faith as I've just expounded it but the willing suppression of inconvenient facts or propagation of unsustainable explanations under the guise of scientific enquiry for the sake of a political programme or creed. The racist nonsense which has sometimes been preached in the name of 'Social Darwinism' is one obvious example, and much of what passed for 'social science' in Eastern Europe under Communism another. It's as self-evident an abuse as forgery or plagiarism even if, as with them, it can for some people in some contexts be justified by the light of some overriding moral imperative of their own. Usually, those who are guilty of it are guilty of bad faith too, because they pretend to their readers that they aren't doing, illocutionarily, what they are. But sometimes, like the Parisian students of the 1960s whose slogan was 'better wrong with Sartre than right with Aron', they are perfectly open about it – which may make it better or worse, depending on your own moral point of view.

There's nothing in any of this which would come as a surprise to Marx or Weber or Durkheim, or for that matter to Herodotus or Confucius or Aristotle. Weber, near the end of his life, gave a lecture to a student audience in Munich about the vocation of *Wissenschaft* – the German word which covers what we call 'scholarship' as well as what we call 'science'. The lecture is almost uncanny in the similarity of what it depicts to what was, as it turned out, to be the experience of any number of university teachers in Britain, and not only in Britain, half a century later. It's all there: the low starting salaries, the conflict of priorities between teaching and research, the promotion of mediocrities over the heads of more gifted candidates for chairs, the lecturers who regard their ability to attract an audience as proof of intellectual distinction, the desire of students to be inspired rather than instructed, the intrusion into the lecture-room of irrelevant and conflicting political convictions, the widespread hostility to science as inimical to a proper feeling for nature, and – which cannot fail to strike home to readers who are sociologists themselves – the awareness not only that a serious and lasting contribution is extraordinarily difficult to achieve in any field of *Wissenschaft* but that it's virtually impossible for sociologists, since they are too unspecialized to do much more than reformulate questions to which only specialists will be able to furnish anything approaching a definitive answer.[5]

This is not, however, a plea for sympathy. The joys and sorrows of the academic life are much like those of any other profession, and the difficulties which stand in the way of the aspiring entrant are not insurmountable now any more than they were then. However dismaying it may be to the practitioners of sociology, or of any other academic discipline, to see the results of their labours misrepresented, ignored, or put to uses which they themselves deplore, the remedy is publicly to expose such conduct for what it is. More threatening, where it occurs, is abuse in the other sense of that word – the invective of those who would like disinterested research to be not so much *perverted* as *subverted* to the point of destruction. The forced closure of universities and schools, the censorship of publications, the prohibition of enquiries which rulers find unpalatable, the burning of books, and the imprisonment or even execution of dissident intellectuals can all be documented for this century just as they can for many others in the past. It would be apocalyptic, not to say paranoid, to suggest that the sociology departments and research institutes of Britain or the United States are seriously threatened by such measures in the year 1998. But it would be naive to deny that Weber's conception of *Wissenschaft* has its enemies not only without but within. Governments, even in so-called liberal democracies, may succumb to the urge to interfere, where they can, in what is studied and taught, while there is at the same time no lack of aspirants to academic positions who will, if *they* can, use them to undermine for *their* political purposes the traditional standards which Weber proclaims. How far they are to be morally reprehended on that account is up to you. But the source of anti-intellectualism in general, and of hostility to sociological research in particular, is one of the topics which sociologists of sociology cannot but address. Nor is it, in its lighter any more than its more sinister manifestations, a feature only of the present day. 'Culture wars', as they are nowadays called, are as old as academia itself, and the motives of the warriors likewise. In the words of a masque performed in the University of Cambridge in 1646:

> Wee'l drive the Doctors out of doores
> And Arts what'ere they be;
> Wee'l cry both Arts, and Learning down,
> And, hey! then up goe we . . .[6]

But what about the *uses* – the 'good' uses, that is? Aren't there legitimate applications of sociology to questions of social policy, even if they still leave room for argument over whether the policy itself is morally right or wrong?

That question reminds me of the question put to me years ago by a pupil of mine called Scotland who, truth being as usual stranger than fiction, played full-back for Scotland. The first thing he said to me was 'Sociology's the same as socialism, isn't it?', to which my immediate reaction was one of slack-jawed dismay. But then I reminded myself of Sidney and Beatrice Webb and R. H. Tawney's *Equality* and *The Aquisitive Society* and the Fabian Society's unrelenting output of reformist pamphlets. I thought about the founding of the British Sociological Association in 1903 and the curious collection of eugenicists, urban planners, charity organizers, social statisticians, and all-purpose do-gooders which it brought together.[7] And I totted up the number of my own academic colleagues whose researches into Britain's class structure, trade unions, educational system, political parties and so forth were unmistakably connected with their lifelong allegiance to the British Labour Party. Young Mr Scotland's question then didn't seem so misconceived after all. Indeed, his view of the matter was not, I concluded, all that far from the view not only of many Conservative politicians but of many American sociologists, to whom twentieth-century British sociology has often seemed only marginally distinguishable from a draft of the social policy section of the Labour Party's manifesto for the next general election.

That, of course, is an exaggeration, not to say a caricature. But even if much of British (or American or any other) sociology *is* self-consciously virtuous in inspiration and ameliorative in intent, what's wrong with that? Many successful research programmes in the physical and biological sciences have been motivated by the ambition of the researchers to come up with solutions to practical problems by which the well-being of humanity will be enhanced.

In economics, although Keynes famously said of his eminent prede-
cessor Alfred Marshall that he had been 'too anxious to do good',[8]
he himself was hardly one to talk, given how clearly his own
moral and political concerns are reflected in his theories of money,
investment, savings, unemployment and so forth. We may think
of the 'gentlemen who felt a strong desire to assist in promoting
the progress of social improvement' and accordingly founded the
Manchester Statistical Society in 1833 as a gaggle of hypocritical
amateurs,[9] and find it as difficult to see *Meliora* – the avowedly
Christian journal of the National Association for the Promotion
of Social Science – as a serious academic publication as to see the
old Remington typewriter which I asked you to picture to yourself
in Chapter II as a piece of up-to-the-minute, state-of-the-art communication technology. But the sociological findings of would-be
social reformers stand or fall irrespective of their hopes and desires
that they will make the world a better place.

What's wrong with do-gooder sociology isn't the motives of its
practitioners but their assumptions. As I hope I've convinced you
by now, one of the most valuable lessons that sociology teaches is
how little it can do, or ever will, to predict how the patterns of
roles constitutive of human groups, communities, institutions and
societies are actually going to evolve. Perhaps, if the rulers and
decision-makers of the world, as well as the would-be reformers
advising them, knew more sociology than they do, they would
make better decisions – by which I mean merely that they would
do fewer things whose consequences turned out to be the opposite
of what they originally pretended to themselves and other people.
But I doubt even that. It was at one time fashionable for statesmen
and generals to claim that they had been guided in their decisions
by the lessons of history, and perhaps it might be true that some
of them were helped to achieve their diplomatic or military suc-
cesses by what they had read about the statecraft of Talleyrand at
the Congress of Vienna or the strategy of Pericles in the opening

years of the Peloponnesian War. But they only said so afterwards, not before. It will only make matters worse if decision-makers are going to look to the practitioners of sciences which are inescapably non-predictive for the one thing which they cannot and never will be able to provide.

At the risk of sounding as tedious as any Platitude-Merchant, as opinionated as any Attitude-Merchant, and as priggish as any Eminent Victorian, I venture to suggest that the study of sociology, by showing us just what kind of a social animal we are, can help to disabuse us of the more complacent illusions we might otherwise be tempted to indulge about ourselves. As Pope said about wisdom in general, 'Tis but to know how little can be known, To see all others' faults and feel one's own'. This may seem an odd thing for me to say in view of the unblushing arrogance with which any number of sociologists have foisted their convictions and prescriptions on their readers. Sociologists are no more immune from the besetting academic sin of vanity than the practitioners of any other branch of *Wissenschaft*. But the more we learn about ourselves as social animals the less we find to be vain about. It's not just that we learn to see ourselves as social *animals* – apes, that is, of a particular kind who happen to have evolved relatively large brains and a remarkable capacity for language. Nor is it just that we find very little to justify the claims of those, whether sociologists or not, who want to tell us that they have seen the future and that it works. Nor is it just that the findings of evolutionary psychology, anthropology and sociology alike all confirm the views of moralists down the ages that human beings have an inherent capacity to be aggressive, manipulative and deceitful as well as altruistic, co-operative and frank. Nor is it just that the part played by chance in human affairs is far greater than most of us like to admit. It's that sociology teaches us not only how difficult it is to explain our social behaviour and its variations across the range of cultures and societies but also how little disposed human beings are either to subject their own behaviour to the scrutiny of science or to accept the findings of the researchers who do.

People generally believe what they want to believe, particularly about themselves, and are apt to find the idea of themselves as objects of scientific enquiry unwelcome if not downright alarming. Of all the multifarious uses of language since it evolved among the particular apes from whom we are all descended, objective self-scrutiny is one of the uncommonest to which it has been put. It's a matter of strenuous current debate among biologists, psychologists and linguists whether the most important function of language among our Pleistocene forebears was to exchange practical information which augmented their capacity for survival and the replication of their genes or to facilitate the cultivation and extension of social relationships which will likewise have enhanced their reproductive fitness. But whatever the answer, there is no doubt that the principal use to which language has been put from then until now is, for want of a better word, chat – gossip, rumour, story-telling, scandal-mongering, myth-making, reminiscing, prophesying, bickering, teasing, joking, praising, blaming, congratulating, boasting, insulting, complaining, commiserating and (again for want of a better word) chatting *up*. We pursue our interests in our social relationships, whether we are manipulating and cajoling or bullying and threatening one another, by means of speech-acts whose illocutionary and perlocutionary functions alike have far more to do with getting other people to respond as we wish than with pursuit of the ideal of publicly testable knowledge about ourselves and our social behaviour. What's more, as we can all see for ourselves, chat works. Just look at what human beings are able to persuade one another to do – at the religious creeds and political movements to which they will devote their lives, the disappointments and hardships they will agree to face in the belief that they are on the way to a better future, and the readiness with which they can be recruited to the service of charlatans who know, as Conrad put it in his novel *Nostromo*, that all they need to do to secure a following is to 'flatter their secret desires'. Is it any wonder that sociology should appear so late in the course of human cultural evolution, or that it should meet so much hostility when it does?

Nothing new about that, as I've said already. But the concluding point with which I want to leave you is that only through the practice of sociology and psychology can we hope to understand not only how far but also why Dio Chrysostom, a famously eloquent Stoic philosopher of the first century AD, was right to ask: why oh why are human beings so hard to teach, but so easy to deceive?

NOTES

I · A VERY SOCIAL ANIMAL

1. Aristotle's classic statement of this proverbial idea is his *Politics* (1253a, 29): for a translation and commentary, see Ernest Barker's English language edition, *The Politics of Aristotle*, p. 8.
2. For 'metacultural' universals such as gossip, play, etc., see D. E. Brown, *Human Universals* (1991).
3. Darwin's remark, from one of his early notebooks, was first published in 1974 in H. E. Gruber, ed., *Darwinian Man*, p. 281.
4. For the first appearance of 'meme', see Dawkins, *The Selfish Gene* (1976), p. 206. On cultural evolution, see Robert Boyd and Peter F. Richerson, *Culture and the Evolutionary Process* (1983). Boyd and Richerson don't like 'meme', because they think it presupposes that information affecting phenotype is transmitted in discrete particles; but their own analysis of cultural evolution is entirely compatible with the broader definition.
5. Cohen's 'Law of Prediction', together with his equally memorable 'Law of Information' ('97.6 per cent of all statistics are made up. Of course, the Law of Information applies to itself'), are set out in his *How Many People can the Earth Support?* (1996), pp. 134 and 21.
6. On infantry drill, see William H. McNeill, *The Pursuit of Power* (1983), ch. 4.
7. I owe the article by Goldstone to Timur Kuran, *Private Truths, Public Lies* (1995), pp. 344–5.

II · WHAT EXACTLY DO YOU WANT TO KNOW?

1. Herodotus's remark comes from Book III, para. 38 of his *Histories*, with particular reference to the Egyptians. Needless to say, his whole enterprise has been very differently interpreted by rival scholars, ranging from the suggestion that he was on a spying mission for Athens to the view that he sat at home and made it all up. See Wilfred Nippel, 'Facts and fictions: Greek ethnography and its legacy', *History and Anthropology* vol. 9 (1996).

2. For a sense of just how much those late Roman bureaucrats *were* like 'ours', see A. H. M. Jones, *The Later Roman Empire 284–602*, II (1964), ch. 16, drawing on the vivid account in John the Lydian's *De Magistratibus Populi Romani* of just about every stereotyped failing of bureaucracy that you can think of, including unnecessary form-filling, inter-departmental jealousy, and the impossibility of firing incompetents who have been promoted by seniority rather than merit.

3. The disconcerting mistake about the Ashanti Queen Mother is reported by Rattray in his *Ashanti* (1923), p. 84.

4. The criticial reappraisal of Margaret Mead's *Coming of Age in Samoa* (1928) is Derek Freeman, *Margaret Mead and Samoa: the making and unmaking of an anthropological myth* (1983). The furore which it caused was predictable enough. But who would have expected it to reach the point that a play should be written about it – David Williamson's *Heretic*? In the words of the publicity leaflet for the play, 'Did the Samoans live, as Mead contended, in a carefree, guiltless, promiscuous paradise? Or is Freeman correct in his assertion that Mead's work, indeed the social thinking of the past several decades, was based on innocent lies?' A measured assessment by someone who has actually looked at Mead's field-notes in the Library of Congress is Martin Orans, *Not Even Wrong: Margaret Mead, Derek Freeman, and the Samoans* (1996).

5. I owe Captain Blair to Morton H. Fried, *The Evolution of Political Society* (1967), p. 86.

6. Sahlins's *How 'Natives' Think – about Captain Cook, for example* (1995) was provoked by Obeyesekere's *The Apotheosis of Captain Cook* (1992).

7. Skorupski's article is 'The Meaning of Another Culture's Beliefs', in C. Hookway and P. Pettit, eds., *Action and Interpretation: Studies in the Philosophy of the Social Sciences* (1978).

8. For Evans-Pritchard's adaptation to witchcraft beliefs and the poison oracle, see his *Witchcraft, Oracles and Magic among the Azande* (1937), pp. 65 and 270.

9. There survives the text of a contract sworn under oath in the church of St Martin at Honfleur by two English 'esquires' on 12 July 1421 to go hostage for each other in the event of capture and ransom and, conversely, to pool any spoils of war. The whole document is printed by K. B. McFarlane, 'A Business Partnership in War and Administration 1421– 1445', *English Historical Review* vol. 78 (1963).

10. Braudel, *The Mediterranean and the Mediterranean World in the Age of Philip II* (Eng. trans., 1972), II, p. 786.

11. Lockwood's article 'Social Integration and System Integration' is reprinted as an Appendix to his *Solidarity and Schism* (1992).

12. On nineteenth-century Haiti, see David Nicholls, *From Dessalines to Duvalier* (1979); for Mamluk Egypt, see Robert Irwin, *The Middle East in the Middle Ages* (1986).

13. On primates, see e.g. F. de Waal, *Chimpanzee Politics* (1982), R. Byrne and A. Whiten, eds, *Machiavellian Intelligence* (1988), D. L. Cheney and R. M. Seyfarth, *How Monkeys See the World* (1990), and S. T. Parker, R. W. Mitchell and M. L. Boccia, eds, *Self-awareness in Animals and Humans* (1994).

14. Geertz's 'Anti-anti-relativism' was published in *American Anthropologist* vol. 86 (1984).

15. Geertz's classic description of Balinese cockfights is reprinted in his *Interpretations of Culture* (1972), ch. 15.

16. For Wittgenstein on 'seeing as', see Pt II, sec xi of his *Philosophical Investigations* (1953).

17. On the unreliability of Russell's own account of his life, see Ray Monk, *Bertrand Russell* (1997).

18. On the automobile industry, see e.g. M. T. Hannan, G. R. Carroll, E. A. Dundon and J. C. Torres, 'Organizational Evolution in a Multinational Context: Entries of Automobile Manufacturers in Belgium, Britain, France, Germany, and Italy', *American Sociological Review* vol. 60 (1995).

19. On the political history of Madagascar, see Maurice Bloch, 'The Disconnection between Power and Rank as a Process: an Outline of the Development of Kingdoms in Central Madagascar', *Archives Européennes de Sociologie* vol. 18 (1977).

20. On the ritual of circumcision, see Bloch's *From Blessing to Violence* (1986).

21. Derrida's italicized remark in the original is in *De la grammatologie* (1967), p. 232: '*La pensée de cette opposition entre la philosophie et l'empirisme n'est pas simplement empirique.*'

III · A CATALOGUE OF ERRORS

1. For the article confirming Aristotle's hypothesis by Roberto Perotti ('Growth, Income Distribution, and Democracy: What the Data Say'), see *The Economist* of 19 October 1996.

2. For ideas as 'switchmen', see 'The Social Psychology of the World Religions', in H. H. Gerth and C. Wright Mills, eds, *From Max Weber* (1947), p. 280.

3. Aron's remark is in his *Main Currents in Sociological Thought* (Eng. trans., 1967), II, p. 245.

4. Evans-Pritchard's remark about Durkheim is in his *Nuer Religion* (1956), p. 313. For a more extended criticism, see his *Theories of Primitive Religion*

(1965), pp. 53–69; but he does allow (p. 100) that for all its faults Durkheim's book will continue to be read as a 'classic'.

5. On Spencer's spectacular success in the United States, see Richard Hofstadter, *Social Darwinism in American Thought* (2nd edn, 1955), ch. 2.

6. Parsons's later view is summarized in *Societies* (whose subtitle, incidentally, is 'Evolutionary and Comparative Perspectives'), p.v.

7. For Leach on the Jinghpaw, see his *Rethinking Anthropology* (1961), p. 50.

8. For Merleau-Ponty's 'universal code of structures', see his *Signs* (Eng. trans., 1964), p. 118.

9. J. B. Watson, *Behaviorism* (1925), p. 82.

10. For 'skyhooks', see Dennett's *Darwin's Dangerous Idea: Evolution and the Meanings of Life* (1995), p. 76.

11. Chomsky's devastating review of Skinner appeared in *Language* vol. 35 (1959).

12. Homans's best-known book is *The Human Group* (1950). See also his *Social Behavior: Its Elementary Forms*, first published in 1961. In the revised edition of 1974, 'Gone is the old Chapter 2 on the behavioral psychology of the pigeon. I concluded that the argument would be put as effectively and more economically if it started right out with the behavioral psychology of humans' (p. v).

13. Mayhew's indignant rejoinder to Mills is in the 'Introduction' to his *Talcott Parsons. On Institutions and Social Evolution* (1982), p. 58.

14. Black's comments are on pp. 283 and 288 of his 'Some Questions about Parsons' Theories' in *The Social Theories of Talcott Parsons: A Critical Examination* (1961), edited by himself.

15. The quotation from Bourdieu is taken from his *Outline of a Theory of Practice* (Eng. trans., 1977), p. 78.

16. Collins's plaintive remark is from his 'Sociology: Proscience or Antiscience?', *American Sociological Review* vol. 54 (1989), p. 137.

IV · POWER

1. The two sentences are taken from Arthur A. Joyce and Marcus Winter, 'Ideology, Power, and Urban Society in Pre-Hispanic Oaxaca', *Current Anthropology* vol. 37 (1996), p. 34.

2. The diagram comes from p. 284 of Lenski's *Power and Privilege* (1966).

3. Phelps Brown's 1979 Joan Woodward memorial lecture, 'The Inequalities of Earnings – an Unexplained Uniformity', was delivered at, and published by, Imperial College, London.

4. Lapière published the results of his experiment in 'Attitudes vs. Action', *Social Forces* vol. 13 (1934).

5. I owe King Ardeshir's categorization of his social inferiors to Reuben Levy, *The Social Structure of Islam* (1962), p. 69.

6. Kiernan, *The Pol Pot Regime: Race, Power, and Genocide in Cambodia under the Khmer Rouge, 1975–79* (1996), p. 464.

7. For the Shilluk *reth*, see Evans-Pritchard's 'The Divine Kingship of the Shilluk of the Nilotic Sudan', in his *Essays in Social Anthropology* (1962).

8. For the contrast between Polynesian 'big-men' and Hawaiian 'paramounts', see Sahlins's article, 'Poor Man, Rich Man, Big Man, Chief: Political Types in Melanesia and Polynesia', *Comparative Studies in Society and History* vol. 5 (1962–3).

9. On the archaeological evidence for early violence, see Laurence H. Keeley, *War before Civilization* (1996), pp. 36–9.

10. See Knauft's article 'Reconsidering Violence in Simple Societies', *Current Anthropology* vol. 28 (1987).

11. Coleman's remark comes from *Foundations of Social Theory* (1990), p. 197.

12. For the Asch experiment, see Solomon E. Asch, *Social Psychology* (1952), ch. 16. For the Milgram experiment, see Stanley Milgram, *Obedience to Authority* (1974), chs 2 and 3.

13. The article 'On the Inadequacy . . .' is by Michael Hechter in Karen S. Cook and Margaret Levi, eds, *The Limits of Rationality* (1990).

14. See Harold Garfinkel, *Studies in Ethnomethodology* (1967).

V · MATTERS OF CHANCE

1. For a sociological view of the causes and consequences of the French Revolution, see W. G. Runciman, 'Unnecessary Revolution: the Case of France', *Archives Européennes de Sociologie* vol. 24 (1983).

2. On the origin of the kilt, see Hugh Trevor-Roper, 'The Invention of Tradition: The Highland Tradition of Scotland', in Eric Hobsbawm and Terence Ranger, eds, *The Invention of Tradition* (1983).

3. Ellul's comment on Sartre's remark comes from his *The Technological Society* (Eng. trans., 1965), p. 206.

4. The exchange between the Minister and the Lord Chief Justice on 27 January 1997 is reported in Parliamentary Debates (Hansard), House of Lords, vol. 577, no. 44.

5. I owe both the blip and its explanation to Chris Nuttall, an old friend and fellow graduate student at the University of California in 1962–3 who became head of statistics in the British Home Office.

6. For the self-satisfied students and teachers, see Robert H. Frank and Philip J. Cook, *The Winner-Take-All Society* (1995), p. 104.

7. The quotation is from Wrangham and Peterson, *Demonic Males* (1996), p. 50.

VI · STRUCTURES AND CULTURES

1. Marx's *Contribution to the Critique of Political Economy* was first translated into English from the second German edition in 1904. The famous two sentences can be found in several anthologies, e.g. Lewis S. Feuer, *Marx and Engels: Basic Writings on Politics and Philosophy* (1959), p. 85, or T. B. Bottomore and M. Rubel, *Karl Marx: Selected Writings in Sociology and Social Philosophy* (1956), p. 52.

2. The quotations from Bloch's *Feudal Society* (Eng. trans., 1961) are from pp. xviii and xx.

3. Wickham's strictures on my attempt at taxonomy are in his review article 'Systactic Structures: Social Theory for Historians', *Past & Present* no. 132 (1991).

4. The table in Giddens's *Sociology* is on p. 43 in the 2nd edition of 1993.

5. Khazanov's disclaimer is on p. 4 of his *Nomads and the Outside World* (Eng. trans., 1983), p. 4.

6. Charlemagne's perceptive exercise in what might be called autosociology is preserved in the Nijmegen Capitulary of March 806, printed in A. Borétius, ed., *Monumenta Germaniae Historica. Legum Sectio II. Capitularia Regum Francorum* (1883), p. 131.

7. Parsons's 1970 article was published in Edward O. Laumann, ed., *Social Stratification: Research and Theory for the 1970s* (1970).

8. On the Aztec war-machine, see John Keegan, *A History of Warfare* (1993), pp. 106–14.

9. On 'Modern Times', see Edmund Wilson, *To the Finland Station* (1940), p. 105.

10. The enormous yams are cited by Boyd and Richerson in *Culture and the Evolutionary Process*, p. 269, from W. R. Bascom, 'Ponapae prestige economy', *Southwestern Journal of Anthropology* vol. 4 (1948).

11. I owe Janson and Goldsmith's article 'Predicting Group Size in Primates: Foraging Costs and Predation Risks', *Behavioral Ecology* vol. 6 (1995), to Wrangham and Peterson, *Demonic Males*, pp. 168–9.

12. On the *Burakumin*, see George de Vos and Hiroshi Wagatsuma, eds, *Japan's Invisible Race* (1966), and Mikiso Hane, *Peasants, Rebels and Outcastes: the Underside of Modern Japan* (1982).

13. The remarks in Thompson's Preface to *The Making of the English Working Class* (1964) are on pp. 11 and 12.

14. See E. A. Wrigley and R. S. Schofield, *The Population of England 1541–*

1871: A Reconstruction (1981). A social history which gives due recognition to demographic trends and influences as well as to subjective experiences is Keith Wrightson's *English Society 1580–1680* (1982).

15. Whyte's claim is made on p. xxii of *Street Corner Society* (1943).

16. Goffmann's footnote on office parties is on p. 97 of his *Asylums* (1961).

17. On sharecropping and its different functions in different environments, see A. F. Robertson, 'On Sharecropping', *Man* vol. 15 (1980).

18. On 'Selective Victorianism', see ch. 1 of Burn's *The Age of Equipoise* (1964).

19. See p. 402 of *The Spears of Twilight* (Eng. trans., 1996).

20. *The Spears of Twilight*, p. 409.

21. *The Spears of Twilight*, p. 194.

VII · HISTORY

1. For the quotations from the *Anglo-Saxon Chronicle*, see Dorothy Whitelock, ed., *English Historical Documents*, I (2nd edn, 1979), p. 173.

2. A useful recent corrective to Eurocentric views of world economic history is Jack Goody, *The East in the West* (1996).

3. *The Roman Revolution* (1939), p. 46. The date of its publication is, incidentally, worth noting: Syme's Octavian is not a little reminiscent of Mussolini.

4. *The Roman Revolution*, p. 227.

5. Disraeli's remark is from ch. 23 of his novel *Contarini Fleming* (1832).

6. The quotation from Roberts is on p. 181 of *The Hutchinson History of the World* (1976).

7. Bloch's remark on multiple fealties is on p. 212 of *Feudal Society*.

8. M. I. Finley, *The Ancient Economy* (1973), p. 83.

9. T. C. Smout, *A History of the Scottish People 1560–1830* (1969), p. 169.

10. The letter of 1645 from Downing to Winthrop is quoted by Winthrop D. Jordan, *White over Black* (1968), p. 69.

11. On resistance to the practice of wage-labour in Buganda, see John Iliffe, *The Emergence of African Capitalism* (1983), pp. 17, 29.

12. Dwight Heath, 'New Patrons for Old: Changing Patron–Client Relationships in the Bolivian Yungas', *Ethnology* vol. 12 (1973).

13. On the rise of owner-occupier housing in Britain, see Peter Saunders, *A Nation of Home-owners* (1990).

VIII · UPS AND DOWNS

1. For Anthony Heath's calculation, see his *Social Mobility* (1981), p. 77.

2. For the Roman consuls, see Keith Hopkins, *Death and Renewal* (1983),

p. 135, and for the Chinese civil servants, E. A. Kracke Jr, *Civil Service in Early Sung China 860–1067* (1953), p. 69.

3. On the misleading self-representation of the early French nobility, see Alexander Murray, *Reason and Society in the Middle Ages* (1978), pp. 91–4.

4. On status discrimination and 'passing' in Ancient Rome, see Z. Yavetz, 'Plebs Sordida', *Athenaeum* vol. 43 (1965).

5. On 'Sanskritization', see M. N. Srinivas, *Religion and Society among the Coorgs of South Asia* (1952).

6. The article by Merton and Rossi is reprinted in Merton's *Social Theory and Social Structure* (2nd edn, 1957), ch. 8.

7. The two quotations from British schoolchildren are taken from Peter Willmott, *Adolescent Boys of East London* (1966), p. 80, and Brian Jackson and Dennis Marsden, *Education and the Working Class* (1962), p. 96.

8. K. Roberts *et al.*, *The Fragmentary Class Structure* (1977), p. 81.

9. The quotation from Goldthorpe is on p. 246 of *Social Mobility and Class Structure in Modern Britain* (1980).

10. John Osborne's remark is from his *A Better Class of Person* (1981), p. 26.

11. Bevin's remark about himself is quoted by Alan Bullock, *The Life and Times of Ernest Bevin*, I (1967), p. 103.

IX · POSSIBLE AND IMPOSSIBLE WORLDS

1. On 'perfect' mobility, see D. V. Glass and J. R. Hall, 'Social Mobility in Great Britain: A Study of Inter-Generation Changes in Status', in D. V. Glass, ed., *Social Mobility in Britain* (1954), pp. 188–98.

2. The Webbs' hope was expressed at p. 196, note 1 of the second edition of *Industrial Democracy*.

3. In the second edition of *Walden Two*, published in 1976, Skinner does say in his Preface (p. viii): 'It is true that when the behavioral sciences have gone beyond the collection of facts to recommend courses of action and have done so by predicting consequences, they have not been too helpful.'

4. Petrarch on Venice is quoted by J. R. Hale, 'Venice and its Empire', in Jane Martineau and Charles Hope, eds, *The Genius of Venice 1500–1600* (1983), p. 11.

5. Macaulay's New Zealander appeared in his review essay of 1840 on Ranke's *History of the Popes*.

6. See Luigi Luca and Francesco Cavalli-Sforza, *The Great Human Diasporas* (Eng. trans., 1995), p. 124.

X · USES AND ABUSES

1. On the twentieth-century 'geoscience revolution', see John A. Stewart, *Drifting Continents and Conflicting Paradigms* (1990); and for earlier paradigm shifts in geology, M. J. S. Rudwick, *The Great Devonian Controversy* (1985) and C. C. Gillispie, *Genesis and Geology* (1969).

2 Westergaard and Resler, *Class in a Capitalist Society* (1975), pp. 109–10.

3. For Austin's three 'speech-acts', see his *How to Do Things with Words*, originally given as lectures at Harvard in 1955 but only published in 1962 after his premature death.

4. Julien Benda's *Le trahison des clercs* was originally published in 1928; it has been translated into English in 1928 as *The Great Betrayal* and in 1969 as *The Treason of the Intellectuals*.

5. Weber's lecture is translated in Gerth and Mills's *From Max Weber*, pp. 129–56.

6. The quotation from 'The Shepheard's Oracles' by Francis Quarles is from Laurence and Helen Fowler, *Cambridge Commemorated: An Anthology of University Life* (1984), p. 87.

7. On the beginnings of the British Sociological Association, see R. J. Halliday, 'The Sociological Movement, the Sociological Society, and the Genesis of Academic Sociology in Britain', *Sociological Review* vol. 16 (1968).

8. Keynes's remark about Marshall is in his *Essays in Biography* (1933), p. 175.

9. I owe the reference to the Manchester Statistical Society of 1833 to Philip Abrams, *The Origins of British Sociology: 1834–1914* (1968), p. 33.

INDEX